Dear Paul,

I thought that you might like a copy of my latest one book!

best wishes Matthew

QUINTESSENTIALLY'S

*100 Most Iconic
Wine Estates*

Alain Graillot ❦ Allegrini ❦ Argiano ❦ Ata Rangi ❦ Au Bon Climat ❦ Auguste Clape
Beaucastel ❦ Bernard Baudry ❦ Billecart-Salmon ❦ Blandy's ❦ Bodegas Hidalgo
Boekenhoutskloof ❦ Bollinger ❦ Castello del Terriccio ❦ Castello di Fonterutoli ❦ Gaierna
M. Chapoutier ❦ Château Ausone ❦ Château Cheval Blanc ❦ Château Climens
Château d'Yquem ❦ Château Haut-Brion ❦ Château Lafite Rothschild
Château Latour ❦ Château Léoville-Las Cases ❦ Château Margaux
Château Petrus ❦ Château Pontet-Canet ❦ Château Rieussec
Château Thivin ❦ Clonakilla ❦ Cloudy Bay ❦ Craggy Range
Cullen ❦ Domaine Armand Rousseau ❦ Domaine Bonneau du Martray
Domaine J-F. Coche-Dury ❦ Domaine Comte Georges de Vogüé
Domaine des Comtes Lafon ❦ Domaine de la Romanée-Conti
Domaine Leflaive ❦ Domaine Méo-Camuzet ❦ Domaine Ponsot
Domaine Ramonet ❦ Domaine Raveneau ❦ Domaine G. Roumier
Domaine René & Vincent Dauvissat ❦ Dr. Loosen
Elio Altare ❦ Etienne Sauzet ❦ Felton Road ❦ Fèlsina ❦ François Cotat
Franz Hirtzberger ❦ Gaja ❦ Georges Vernay ❦ Graham's ❦ Grosset ❦ E. Guigal
Huet ❦ Isole e Olena ❦ Jean-Louis Chave ❦ Joh. Bürgy ❦ J.J. Prüm ❦ Karthäuserhof
La Rioja Alta ❦ La Spinetta ❦ La Taille aux Loups ❦ Le Pin ❦ Leeuwin Estate
Louis Roederer ❦ Marcel Deiss ❦ Miguel Torres ❦ Morà ❦ Oremus ❦ Ornellaia
Pegasus Bay ❦ Penfolds ❦ Peter Lehmann ❦ Pieropan ❦ Planeta ❦ Poderi Aldo Conterno
Pol Roger ❦ Poliziano ❦ Quinta do Noval ❦ Ridge ❦ Rustenberg ❦ Sadie Family
Sassicaia ❦ Shafer ❦ Spottswoode ❦ Taylor's ❦ Tempier ❦ Tyrrell's ❦ Valdespino
Vega Sicilia ❦ Vieux Télégraphe ❦ Vieux Château Certan ❦ Warre's ❦ Wendouée

QUINTESSENTIALLY'S

100 Most Iconic
Wine Estates

CURATED BY
MATTHEW JUKES

QUINTESSENTIALLY
PUBLISHING

Contents

PLEASE NOTE
THE GEOGRAPHICAL ORDER
TAKES ITS STARTING POINT FROM
GREENWICH MEAN TIME MOVING
EASTWARDS ACROSS THE GLOBE.

Introduction

by *Matthew Jukes*

for Amelia

• The challenge I set myself for this book was not simply to find 100 Iconic Estates in the vast world of wine. This would be a doddle. It was, in fact, to whittle down a mighty list of extraordinarily talented wine producers to a perfectly balanced century. This involved some truly brutal battles (on paper) - Château against Château and Domaine against Domaine. It was at times agonising but always great fun, and with the 100 Iconic Estates list complete, I am delighted to present it to you. This list features estates whose wines have electrified my palate since I started working in the wine business 25 years ago. Many, I am sure, will be familiar to you. Others, less so, and I hope that this encourages you to broaden your vinous horizons.

The wine world is ever-changing, but these estates can be relied upon to make stellar wines year in, year out – they are the shimmering bedrock of the wine world. Showcasing an incredible array of grape varieties, regions and countries, with hypnotic aromas and devastating flavours there are sublime creations on every page. All are unique, celebrating their exact position on our planet and fashioning delicious wines which entrance our senses. A fair few of the pioneers mentioned within these covers have changed the paradigm of winemaking in their sphere. There are wines here that don't cost the earth and that bring great joy; nestling comfortably next to those whose rarity and cost are truly breath-taking. These are also all wines that I would love to have in my own collection; forming the most complete and balanced cellar that I can design.

I hope that my descriptions inspire you to experience what I have tasted and that this drives you to further populate your own wine racks with legendary bottles.

Portugal

* Madeira not to scale

Blandy's

"This company has been a quiet pioneer, gently developing its time-honoured recipes and routes to market for 200 years."

Madeira
Established 1811

|01

• The Blandy's story starts with a mystery. Legend had it that John Blandy, founder of this esteemed Madeira Lodge, came to the island in 1807 as a quartermaster to General Beresford, who was commander of the British garrison charged with protecting Portugal from Napoleon. But his name is not found in any of the army lists of those men based on Madeira. It was not until August 2006 when one Emmanuel 'Mannie' Berk, a Madeira fanatic, unearthed the truth. He discovered a letter sent from London to Messrs Newton, Gordon, Murdoch, wine merchants in Madeira, which immediately solved the family conundrum. It read, 'Sirs! At the desire of our particular friend, Richard Fuller Esq., Banker in this City, we beg leave to introduce Mr John Blandy who visits your Island on account of ill health, and wishes to obtain employment in a Counting House.' The letter was dated 23 December 1807, so it is assumed that John arrived in early 1808 rather than with the British army in 1807. Now that this mystery has been solved my book can start off on a solid footing.

This company has been a quiet pioneer, gently developing its time-honoured recipes and routes to market for 200 years. In 1925, Blandy's decided to join the Madeira Wine Association, a group of wine companies set up to increase global exposure and awareness of the wines at the same time as minimising overheads. Under the guidance of the Blandy

family, this group managed to survive the challenging conditions of World War II while other companies disappeared off the radar.

In 1989, the Blandy family approached another Anglo-Portuguese family, the Symingtons (see the Warre's and Graham's chapters) and they offered them a partnership in the newly named Madeira Wine Company. The Symingtons' worldwide Port contacts introduced Blandy's to a new global audience. For over two decades the Symingtons helped the members of the MWC with marketing and technical expertise and this stood Blandy's, Cossart Gordon, Leacock and Miles Madeiras in good stead. Two hundred years after John Blandy founded his eponymous company in 1811, the Blandy's celebrated their bicentennial by re-acquiring a majority stake in their historic family business.

Today, Michael and Chris Blandy are the 6th and 7th generations to work in their

Madeira business and we are delighted that they have survived this long because the style of wine made here is not only venerable and historic it is also one of the most underrated of all on Earth.

There are three main types of Madeira made and Blandy's is an expert in all styles. The oldest and most sought-after are the Vintage Madeiras which are aged for a minimum of 20 years before bottling. The Colheita wines are aged between eight and 15 years in cask and often represent incredible value for money. The final category is the Blends - which can be five,10,15, 20, 30 and over 40 years old. The four grape varieties used in Madeira are, from driest to sweetest, Sercial, Verdelho, Bual and Malmsey. So combine the grape and its dryness or sweetness with a corresponding age category and, hey presto, you have your wine. This might involve a little bit of to-ing and fro-ing but you will get the hang of it in no time. Madeira seems to be perpetually out of fashion and underrepresented in

restaurants and on dinner tables, but in my experience, my Madeira motto 'once tasted, never forgotten' never fails. Everyone I have poured Madeira for in my wine life has fallen under its spell. It is also the longest lived of any wine style on the planet – so a bottle of birth year Madeira is the perfect gift for someone who thinks that they have everything. Who would have thought that there are such wonderful vinous gems to be found on a little island 600 miles off the Moroccan coast? John Blandy – that's who.

01   *A legendary Blandy's bottle*
02   *A stunning vineyard overlooking*
      the ocean

Graham's

"I will continue to follow the Symingtons' every step because they are phenomenal guardians of this majestic style of wine and their Ports are all utterly captivating."

Douro Valley
Established 1820

01

• W & J Graham's was founded in Oporto in 1820 by brothers William and John Graham. This successful Scottish family was already an established merchant with business dealings in India, but their venture in Portugal was to take them into Port production for the very first time. They focused their efforts on establishing a great brand and to this end they invested in property in the Upper Douro in order to source the finest raw material possible. Graham's purchased Quinta dos Malvedos in 1890 and this masterstroke set the tone for the future. As one of the Douro Valley's finest 'river' Quintas', the quality of their grapes enabled them to make Vintage Port of the very highest order.

In the early 20th century Graham's Vintage Port declarations could not have been more imposing or majestic. I am very fortunate to have tasted some of these wines and they are some of the finest ever made. If ever you are offered the opportunity to taste the 1908, 1912, 1924, 1927, 1945 or 1948 vintages, cancel any prior engagements and, if necessary, cross continents to do so. In the decades that followed however, Graham's has also made other staggering Vintage releases.

These days the range of wines is entirely sublime but this depth of field was introduced when the Symington family bought the operation in 1970. The Symingtons (themselves highly skilled

Port producers) built on the hard work that the Grahams had invested into their brand. Another Scottish family, the Symingtons are descended from Andrew James Symington and Beatrice Atkinson who were married in Oporto in 1891. Miss Atkinson's father and uncle were Port producers and on her mother's side, she is directly related to the 17th century Port merchant, Walter Maynard. Now this is a fabulous point of detail - Maynard is recorded as shipping 39 Pipes of Port to England in 1652. This is one of the oldest shipments of Port ever made by a British merchant. Today five members of the Symington family, the 13th generation in the Port trade, work in the business and they are regarded as one of the most talented and dedicated wine companies in the world. They all own and manage their own vineyards up and down the Douro Valley and these grapes are supplied to their business.

Graham's range starts with a traditional, juicy Ruby, a bright, crunchy, refreshing Tawny and a particularly fine White, but it is a wine called Six Grapes that quickens my pulse. This is one of Graham's original Port marques. The fruit is sourced from the same vineyards that contribute to the great Vintage wine and it wears its heart on its sleeve. Graham's tag line for this wine is, 'everyday Port for the Vintage Port drinker' and this is actually spot on! Once you have acquired a taste for the generous, all-enveloping Graham's style you can graduate to a fragrant LBV and a neat range of Tawnies. Not content with offering the usual 10, 20, 30 and 40-year-old styles there is also a wine called The Tawny, which is one of my favourite chillable Ports for summer drinking. Moving up the scale you encounter Graham's Crusted – an unfiltered, dense, brooding style which requires decanting to remove the thick 'crust', and which imparts hedonistic intensity on the palate. My favourite wine in the line-up, on account of its value and iconic flavour, is the Graham's Quinta dos Malvedos

Vintage Port, coming from the heart of the estate and made in 'undeclared years'. This dreamy creation has all the bravado and class of the Vintage wine, but more tenderness and an earlier drinking window. Finally, at the top of the estate sits the Vintage Port; an intensely powerful yet graceful wine that commands attention and sets it apart from its peers.

I will continue to follow the Symingtons' every step because they are phenomenal guardians of this majestic style of wine and their Ports are all utterly captivating.

01 *The Graham's vintage Port cellar in Oporto*
02 *Grape pickers at Quinta dos Malvedos*

| 02

Warre's

"This house crafts wines which have pronounced aromatics; sleek, but not muscular mid-palates and then fine, crisply acidic finishes."

Douro Valley
Established 1670

| 01

01   *Warre's 1963 Vintage Port*
02   *A Warre vineyard*

• The story of Warre's Port started nearly three and a half centuries ago, in 1670, when two Englishmen, William Burgoyne and John Jackson, opened an office in northern Portugal trading in wine, olive oil and fruit. Over the next 60 years the company evolved as new partners

became involved and in 1729, it became Messrs. Clark, Thornton & Warre, with the arrival of William Warre in Portugal. Warre specialised in Port and by the end of the 18th century they were handling 10% of the total of Port exports.

William's grandson, also named William, was an exceptional man whose fortitude shaped the company's future. He was commissioned as a British army officer and he played a vital role in nearly all of the key battles throughout the Peninsular War (1808 – 1812). Being Porto-born, Captain Warre's knowledge of the language and the country made him invaluable to his commanders, Field Marshall Beresford and the Duke of Wellington. The Duke ordered a hogshead of Port from William's father and, in a letter William noted to his father that 'he does not care about the price' – what a fabulous piece of vinous trivia and it's nice to know that quality is, and always has been, far more important than price! With Napoleon's armies defeated, William received awards for gallantry from both Portugal and England in recognition of his valour. It seems fitting that Warre's Warrior Reserve Port is the first and oldest Port brand in the world, having been shipped continuously since 1750.

The Symington family has a 350-year history in the Port trade and Andrew James Symington was admitted to the partnership of the firm of Warre & Co. in 1905.

Today, Warre's Port is run by the same team who runs Graham's Port (q.v.) and their flagship Quinta is Quinta da Cavadinha, located in the Pinhão Valley, in the upper reaches of the Douro. Like Graham's, each of the family members owns and manages their own Warre's property. With a full range of Port styles, including White, Ruby and Tawny, my favourite starting point is the wine that inspired the whole company in the 18th century, Warrior. Made from fruit from their prestige Quintas, da Cavadinha and do Retiro, this is a mighty, Vintage-shaped wine that costs around the same as a bottle of Sancerre! This further highlights the fact that top flight Port is among the finest value wine you can ever hope to taste. Rising up the ladder you encounter Warre's single vintage Colheita Ports. These are ethereal beasts, made from one declared year, but aged for an extended period in oak, thus tawny in colour and flavour. Rare and savoury, I often think that great Warre's Colheita Ports are similar in dimension to fine, old dry Sherries and you should drink them on the same occasions – as chic aperitifs with charcuterie and fresh crustacea.

So far, so traditional, but one of the Port marketing triumphs of the last two decades came in the form of Otima – a 50cl, cutting-edge 10-year-old Tawny Port, created to bring this engaging style of wine to an audience other than the stereotypical gentleman's club stalwart. This it did with style and a 20-year-old version has been added to the range. Chillable, packaged in a clear bottle and good for any occasion this catapulted Warre's and its other wines back into our collective consciousness. Following on, the sensuous LBV is a mellower creation with complex aromas and a satisfying finish. Warre's Ports are contemplative wines and this is shown beautifully by the vintage, single Quinta release, Quinta da Cavadinha that comes exclusively from one of the finest vineyard estates in the Douro. This style of wine ages superbly but over a shorter overall time span than the Vintage Port, so feel free to dive in after 15 or 20 years.

02

Above this wine is the pinnacle of production, Warre's Vintage Port and while I have never tasted any of the great vintages from the late 1800s, I have it on good authority that they are still sublime. The key to Warre's longevity is their pristine acidity. This house crafts wines which have pronounced aromatics; sleek, but not muscular mid-palates and then fine, crisply acidic finishes. This bright acidity is the battery pack for the wine to age and I would wager that the 1994, 1997, 2000, 2003 and 2007 will all make the century mark if cellared correctly. This would indeed please William Warre.

03 *Close-up views of Warre's vineyards*
04 *Annual Race of the traditional Barco*
     Rabelo Port Boats
05 *Warre's cellars*

Taylor's

"An independent, family owned and run business, the drive and determination seen at Taylor's is directly reflected in their powerful age-worthy wines."

Douro Valley
Established 1692

• Taylor's Port house was established in 1692. As a specialist Port producer, with over 300 years of experience, this house is a veritable treasure trove for the committed Port enthusiast. Taylor's also owns and operates two other famous Port houses in the Douro, Fonseca which it acquired in 1949 and Croft which it bought in 2001. Drawing on fruit from its famous Quinta de Vargellas estate and also the acclaimed vineyards of Quinta de Terra Feita and Quinta do Junco, Taylor's has been able to craft a spectacular range of wines utilising the exact aroma and flavour characteristics from each of its distinctly different geographical locations within the Douro Valley. An independent, family-owned and run business, the drive and determination seen at Taylor's is directly reflected in their powerful age-worthy wines.

While this distinguished estate has three centuries of history under-pinning its name it is the last 50 years which have shaped its modern-day image. In 1966, Richard Yeatman, Chairman and owner of Taylor Fladgate and Fonseca suddenly passed away. His widow, Beryl, asked her nephew, Alistair Robertson, to return to Oporto from working in the wine business in the UK, to assume management of the firm. This key appointment set Taylor's on a stunning trajectory. Roberston hit upon an idea which transformed the Port market. He produced a style of Port, from a single vintage, that had already been filtered (unlike traditional Vintage Port), so that it

could be drunk, un-decanted, for ease, as soon as it hit the market. Port matures faster if it is left in oak barrels. The leviathan Vintage Port can take two decades to mature and soften because it does its aging very slowly in the bottle. So by keeping the Port in barrel for longer and bottling it later, you could mellow the Port significantly and bring it right up to its drinking window. Taylor's Late Bottled Vintage was launched in 1970 with the 1965 vintage. Nowadays LBV Port is commonplace, but Taylor's pioneered this immensely enjoyable style of Port and it is the only brand which I have written up in my various columns every year, without fail, since I started writing about wine. Back in the 70's this style of Port was viewed somewhat suspiciously by those used to cellaring Port for aeons, but the convenience and affordability of Taylor's LBV, coupled with its true 'Vintage-flavour' soon won people over. With the Taylor's name buzzing they became market leaders in another style: aged Tawny Port. Taylor's cleverly built up significant reserves of fine, cask-aged Tawnies. This forward-thinking

manoeuvre was to pay great dividends when, in 1973, the Instituto do Vinho do Porto, created new rules allowing producers to write the age of the Tawny Ports on the labels. Taylor's was the first major house to take advantage of this change in regulations, launching a full range of 10, 20, 30 and 40-year-old Tawnies.

In 1994, Alistair's eldest daughter Natasha and her husband Adrian Bridge moved to Oporto and they joined the family company. Funnily enough I knew Adrian long before he met the Robertsons because he was my House Captain at school back in 1980. I am indebted to him for two things – teaching me how to kick a rugby ball and introducing me to Taylor's (both crucial in a young man's repertoire!). He was inspirational at 17, so when I heard that he became MD of one of the most important Port houses in 2000 it didn't surprise me at all. With Natasha as Chief Blender, this is a very talented couple indeed. Under Adrian's dynamic leadership and with the talented David Guimaraens as winemaker

the company has gone from strength to strength. Quinta de Terra Feita, Quinta de Vargellas and the ultra-rare Vargellas Vinha Velha, not forgetting the Classic Vintage and the aforementioned Tawnies and LBV, make up one of the most impressive portfolios in the wine world.

01 *Taylor's Quinta de Vargellas*
02 *Breathtaking vineyards*

Quinta do Noval

"Quinta do Noval is a guiding light with a powerful portfolio of wines imbued with passion and integrity."

Douro Valley
Established 1715

| 01

01   *Quinta do Noval Vintage 2003*
02   *Quinta do Noval's spectacular estate,*
      including the fabled Nacional vineyard,
      perched high above the Douro Valley

• The most expensive bottle of port that I ever bought was the legendary 1931 Quinta do Noval Nacional. As wine buyer for Bibendum Restaurant in London, with Sir Terence Conran as a director, it seemed fitting to source this incredible, birth-year wine for him as a present for his 60th. I am assured that it is a life-changing potion. The fact that this port superstar has hung its reputation off this extraordinary, ungrafted wine is remarkable enough but it's the changes that occurred long after it was made that have secured QdN's position in this glorious century.

Back in 1715, this property was gifted by the Prime Minister, Marquês de Pombal, to the Rebello Valente family, later passing by marriage to Viscount Vilar D'Allen. Disaster struck in 1880 though when the phylloxera bug struck, destroying many of the property vineyards and those of the Douro estates. This downturn forced Quinta do Noval onto the market and it was bought in 1894 by António José da Silva. Da Silva's visionary talents prompted him immediately to set about replanting the vineyards and renovating the property. His inspired efforts, widening the terraces to maximise sun exposure can still be seen today. This work lived on through his son-in-law Luiz Vasconcelos Porto and his declaration of the 1931 Vintage Nacional - made from vines that had dodged the phylloxera bullet - catapulted Noval onto the global stage. Only three shippers declared in 1931 and so Noval's rarity coupled with its unquestionable quality set this historic estate up forever. Noval has pioneered stencilled bottles, aged Tawny ports and even the Late Bottled Vintage style. In 1981 a raging inferno destroyed

Noval's lodge, bottling plant and offices in Vila Nova de Gaia. Two hundred years of records were lost along with 20,000 bottles of the 1978 vintage and 350,000 litre of stock. A year later Porto's great grandchildren, Cristiano and Teresa Van Zeller took over, built a vast lodge at Quinta do Noval and continued to spread the word about their delicious wines. In 1993 the Van Zeller family sold Noval to the insurance group AXA, which had extensive interests in Bordeaux, owning Châteaux Pichon-Baron, Petit-Village and Suduiraut, as well as Hungary's Tokaj producer Disznókő. Englishman Christian Seely was appointed MD of Noval and eight years later he was promoted to MD of the entire AXA Millésimes portfolio.

His vision and faith in the winemaker António Agrellos has led to a third renaissance for this illustrious port house and another wave of replanting and renovation. Thanks to changes in regulations, port could now be shipped from the Douro rather than from Vila Nova de Gaia and so Seely orchestrated the installation of a bottling line and a new warehouse, making it the first traditional shipping company to move its operations to the Douro.

A 145ha property, with nearly half of its replanting less than a decade old, Quinta do Noval is now set for the 21st century. The Nacional plot is just 2.5ha and only produces 250 cases when it is declared in special years, but the rest of the portfolio is equally as captivating with every single bottle oozing class, distinction and a profound respect for its origins. From Noval Black, the stunningly packaged, black-fruit soaked entry level port, via the celestial, unfiltered single vineyard LBV, to a singular Vintage port called Silval and culminating in the mighty Vintage Port itself, Quinta do Noval inspires the drinker every step of the way. Add 10, 20 and 40-year-old Tawnies and a stunning Vintage Colheita into the creative mix and the depth of field is extended. The strength and distinction of the red wines made at Noval is even more remarkable with Quinta do Noval DOC and Cedro do Noval, both Douro reds leading the field. Far from being a one-wine estate created nearly a century ago, Quinta do Noval is a guiding light with a powerful portfolio of wines imbued with passion and integrity.

Spain

Bodegas Hidalgo

"Javier is a local hero and in my eyes he is the market leader in one of the most delicious and under-appreciated white wine styles in existence."

Sanlúcar de Barrameda
Established 1792

• Established in 1792, the family-owned Hidalgo Sherry business is now in its sixth generation and it is the region's definitive Manzanilla house. I will never forget flying down to Sanlúcar de Barrameda to meet Javier Hidalgo and to visit his ancient winery. It seemed to me that nothing had changed in two centuries, as I tasted and toured the incredible facility. With extensive vineyard holdings, on the famed albariza soils of the region, coupled with an impressive bodega in the centre of the town, Javier is a local hero and in my eyes he is the market leader in one of the most delicious and under-appreciated white wine styles in existence – Manzanilla Sherry. His world-famous brand La Gitana (the 'gypsy' depicted on the label) is a sensational wine, sold at an everyday price-point. I think that you have to drink La Gitana in Sanlúcar, with mountains of local tapas to really understand why it is such a magnificent elixir. Once you have done this you will most likely have a bottle stationed permanently in your fridge.

Allow me a moment of indulgence if you will. There is no other alcoholic drink on Earth that can complement let alone romance such a wide range of irresistible dishes. Fabulous salted almonds, steamed butterfly clams, juicy garlic prawns, sturdy patatas bravas, mouth-watering salt cod fritters, hot pimentos de pardon, succulent tomato bread, dense Spanish tortilla, heady Iberico ham, intense pickled anchovies, heavenly empanadas, aromatic charred

octopus, tender pork and beef meatballs in tomato sauce, croquettes and chicken livers in sherry to name but a few. Even Sushi, Thai, Indonesian and lighter Indian food works incredibly well with it, too. The enviable, ultra-classy and yet affordable Spanish grazing tradition is such an attractive way of eating, chatting, drinking and valuing every second of life, and it is clearly not just the Spanish that have the market share of this socially inclusive existence.

Beyond the famous La Gitana brand is a veritable treasure trove of other Sherries. I will point out my favourite before delving into the more structured styles. Pasada Pastrana is an aged single vineyard Manzanilla – if you like the Grand Cru version of La Gitana. The Palomino grape performs at its finest in the Miraflores district and this wine, from the single vineyard of Pastrana, is the pinnacle of production. Despite its perfection on the nose and palate, this is one of the least expensive and yet mesmerising wines in

this book. Javier is justly proud of Pastrana and it's a mystery to me why it is not sold by the glass, as an Elysian aperitif wine, in every serious restaurant in the world.

Javier's Premium range includes four further styles: a rich, dry and nutty Napoleón Amontillado (named after the man himself – Hidalgo's wines fortified some of Napoleon's campaigns); an extraordinarily smooth Oloroso Seco Faraón (the faraón is the head of a gypsy family); a figgy, sweet Alameda Cream Sherry (named after the central plaza in Seville where young men would loiter in the hope of finding a date) and Triana Pedro Ximénez a sweet and raisin-like potion for ice cream and toffee puddings (named after one of Columbus's shipmates who first spied America).

Beyond this range you will find the VOS (20+ year-old Very Old Sherry) and the VORS (30+ year-old Very Old Rare Sherry) wines. Here you will discover Jerez Cortado Wellington (to balance the aforementioned

Napoleón and, yes, Hidalgo sold wine to both sides during the wars!). These are stunning old wines drawn from ancient casks and they are some of the most remarkable creations that I have ever tasted.

Javier's other passion is horse racing, and one of the most exciting events in the calendar is the Carreras de Caballos Sanlúcar dating back to 1845. This festival of racing in August, in which horses sprint down two kilometres of beach at the mouth of the Río Guadalquivir, is incredible. I saw Javier win his race one year and he celebrated by buying everyone an ice cold glass of La Gitana – yet another occasion to enjoy a glass of Manzanilla.

01   *The iconic image for La Gitana*
02   *D.O. Jerez, vineyards in the Miraflores district*

Valdespino

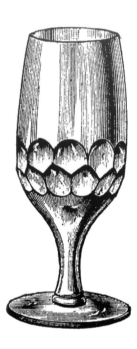

• Valdespino Sherries are among the best value wines in the world. Deliciosa is the strident, energetic Manzanilla in the pack and Inocente is the mouth-watering, tangy Fino. Tio Diego is a very serious Amontillado and the old Don Gonzalo Amontillado label has been re-released in the VOS range of older Solera-style wines. The prize for the best name and label though goes to Contrabandista, a medium-dry Amontillado sweetened with a dribble of boozy, raisiny PX.

And finally, the Pedro Ximénez, El Candado is regarded as the finest of its kind. With 700 years of experience making Sherry, I would wager that they have indeed got these wines right and that's why I adore them so much!

Vega-Sicilia

• I was lucky enough to attend a vertical tasting of Vega-Sicilia Unico vintages dating back to 1920. The elegance and grace with which this mighty Ribera del Duero red had aged was captivating. This estate, founded in 1864, makes the most incredible wines in Spain from the Tempranillo variety, known locally as Tinto Fino, also using Cabernet Sauvignon, Merlot, Malbec and possibly Carmenère in the mix. Unbelievably complex and powerful on the palate, these wines need at least 15 years to shed their tannic cloak. A more forward-drinking cuvée, Valbuena 5, is also made here along the same lines as the Grand Vin but from more precocious barrels. In addition to these two classic wines, a modernist's dream, Alión also recruits thousands of acolytes to the cause via its slick, exuberant fruit which is immediately appealing and very showy. Finally, Vega has invested in a significant Rioja property with the Rothschild family, and the two unreleased samples that I tasted were suitably impressive. It seems that everything this wine company touches, including its Hungarian property Oremus (q.v.), turns to gold.

Miguel Torres

"A new dawn for artisanal Spanish wines coupled with world class cooking started to attract global attention – this is the Spain we know today and Torres had played a huge part in its image."

Penedès
Established 1870

| 01

won Man of the Year, Wine Personality of the Year and Lifetime Achievement awards from esteemed publications, but this doesn't stop him putting in the hard yards, travelling widely, interviewing, hosting tastings and passing on his knowledge with alacrity. I was shaking in my boots the very first time I met him, over two decades ago, but I needn't have been worried because he is an utterly engaging mentor. His high standards, tenacious work ethic and fairness in pricing mean that his wines appeal to every palate and every pocket, too. The impeccable attention to detail that goes into every one of his bottles is almost too overwhelming to comprehend.

Founded in 1870 Miguel is the fourth generation to run this family owned business. He has extensive vineyard holdings in Penedès, in his home region of Catalonia, and has also branched out to Priorat, Ribera del Duero, Jumilla, Conca de Barberà, Rioja and Toro – he is Mr. Spain. He also has a very impressive outpost in South America, Miguel Torres Chile, which operates a five-tier portfolio, including the fabulous Santa Digna range. He spotted the Chilean opportunity as long ago as 1979, a decade or so before other 'flying winemakers' started whizzing around the globe and I still find Torres as reliable and pioneering as any other estate in the country. You can be assured of tiptop quality whenever you open a Torres wine be it his inexpensive, crisp, floral Viña Sol white, the enigmatic Viña Esmeralda - most

01   *Miguel Torres' rich range of wines*
02   *Mas La Plana Estate*

• It is hard to know where to start with a subject as talented, influential and iconic as the great Miguel Torres and his exemplary, eponymous wine company. The respect that he commands in the wine industry, globally, is staggering. He may well have

wine lovers' first glimpse at a deliciously exotic, dry white wine - or, Sangre de Toro red, made from Garnacha and Cariñena (Grenache and Carignan in French, i.e. a Côtes-du Rhône taste-alike) which always outperforms entry level Southern French red wines. With over 25 Spanish brands, (these first three are the best value, and they inevitably find their way into my newspaper columns), Torres is also a master craftsman when it comes to rarer cuvées like the cult Grans Muralles made from a single walled vineyard of ancient Spanish grape varieties or the world-famous Cabernet Sauvignon, Mas La Plana. It was this wine, back in 1979 when it was called Black Label, which catapulted Torres into the big time with wine collectors and restaurant wine lists. The 1970 vintage of Black Label trounced a few of the other estates in this book in a blind tasting held in Paris. This not only shone the spotlight on Torres and his beloved Penedès region but also on newer wave, modern, yet authentic Spanish wines. It's

worth remembering that as recently as the early 70s most Spanish wine made left the country in tankers and not bottles. A new dawn for artisanal Spanish wines coupled with world-class cooking started to attract global attention – this is the Spain we know today and Torres had played a huge part in its image.

Torres also houses a mighty Spanish Brandy arm and while we don't see these brandies in great numbers outside of Spain, they are considered to be at the top of the 'digéstif tree'. Torres is a phenomenal operation, headed up by Miguel, but with his daughter, Mireia Torres Maczassek, managing the Priorat and Jean Leon wineries, and his son Miguel Torres Maczassek assuming the role of general manager, (while Miguel Senior remains as group president) you can be sure that this hard-working and family operation will continue to go from strength to strength. No matter where you are in the world, you

shouldn't be too many metres from a bottle of highly professional, authentically sourced and astutely made Torres wine! With an active environmental program that is leading the way in the country, a charitable foundation run by his wife Waltraud which provides schools and shelters all over the world and a sister, Marimar, who runs her own winery in Sonoma County, California, this is a very successful wine family, with a global footprint and a fervently loyal following.

02

La Rioja Alta

• In 1890, five Basque and Rioja-based vine growers created the 'Sociedad Vinicola De La Rioja Alta' in order to make very high quality wines. One year later they changed its name to La Rioja Alta. In 1942 they invented Viña Ardanza – a brand that still makes waves today. In 1970, Viña Arana and Viña Alberdi were added to the fold, and are once again very strong brands today. Throughout the last century, the winery has constantly been upgraded and all of the barrels used are coopered at the property. In addition to the three aforementioned lines, named after three of the founding families, there are two Gran Reserva wines, 904 and 890, with 890 being the pinnacle of production. These are traditional style Riojas with intense cherry, pipe smoke and cedarwood notes on the nose that age amazingly well. The wines of La Rioja Alta are to my mind, the essence of the historic Spanish wine trade.

France

Pol Roger

"Only 1.5 million bottles are made per year and it's not uncommon for the latest vintage releases to sell-out before even reaching the market such is their fame and reputation."

Epernay
Champagne
Established 1849

| 01

01 *Sir Winston Churchill, 1999*
02 *Pol Roger Estate in Epernay*

• Perhaps the most famous anecdotes concerning this eminent and discreet Champagne House are those concerning its connections with Sir Winston Churchill. It is documented that Churchill was a keen admirer of Pol

Roger Champagne. A fan since 1908, it wasn't until a luncheon that was given by the British ambassador to France, Alfred Duff Cooper, after the liberation of Paris, that Churchill met the enchanting Odette Pol-Roger. Photographed by Cecil Beaton and described as 'one of the most beautiful women in Paris', Churchill had a soft spot for Odette and he and his wife Clementine forged a great friendship with her that lasted until his death in 1965. Odette was equally taken with Sir Winston and she sent him a case of vintage Pol Roger (the 1928 that he first tasted in Paris with her, until it ran out and thereafter the best vintage) on his birthday every year. Churchill named one of his racehorses after Pol Roger and he also made sure that Odette was invited to lunch at the British embassy every time he travelled to Paris for meetings.

Pol Roger so valued its connection with Britain's greatest hero that on his death they put black borders on the Champagne labels destined for sale in the UK as a mark of respect. In 1984 Pol Roger went one step further by naming their Prestige Cuvée Sir Winston Churchill, after him. Aged for nearly a decade before release and made in the rich style that Churchill so loved, the first vintage was the spectacular 1975. Churchill noted that, 'Champagne imparts a feeling of exhilaration' and also that, 'nerves are braced, the imagination is equally stirred; the wits become more nimble' when drinking it. This endorsement is about as well-qualified as it gets and I am sure that we all agree with Winston's sentiments.

Now that you know the calibre of person who drinks Pol Roger here is some more background on their story. Founded in 1849 and based in Epernay, this relatively small operation has always kept a low profile. Pol Roger himself came from Aÿ and he worked hard for 50 years to establish his brand. His sons, Maurice and Georges, changed their surname to Pol-Roger by deed poll and three more generations followed. Today the company remains boutique-sized, family-owned and obsessive about the quality of its wines. Pol Roger owns 87ha of vineyards; a very solid base with which to make its sublime cuvées. Only 1.5 million bottles are made per year and it's not uncommon for the latest vintage releases to sell-out before even reaching the market such is their fame and reputation.

With a Royal Warrant awarded by Queen Elizabeth II, Pol Roger is a favourite Champagne with the Royal Family and was served en magnum at Prince William and Catherine Middleton's wedding. There are, in addition, a further six wines all worthy of particular attention. The non-vintage trio of Brut Réserve, Pure and Rich play with varying residual sugar quantities. 'Brut Réserve', in formally known as 'White Foil', is one of the most beautiful wines in the region. Fabulously suave and satisfying it is an aficionado's style of Champagne with a moreish texture and complex flavour palette. 'Pure' is a relatively new incarnation, with no residual sugar whatsoever – this bone dry style is certainly attracting a lot of interest, not least because of its stunning food and wine matching properties with seafood, sushi and crustacea. 'Rich' is a seductive, mellifluous, slightly sweet style which I crave with light puddings. There is a vintage trio, too, for you to dive into. 'Brut Vintage', 'Brut Rosé' and 'Blanc de Blancs' are stunningly built wines with brio, drive and vivacity. These are wines that stir the imagination and at the same time taste uniquely fashioned by Pol Roger. This is why I am such an ardent admirer of the wines from this tremendous House.

02

Billecart-Salmon

"If I had to choose just one bottle from Champagne, this is it."

Mareuil-sur-Aÿ
Champagne
Established 1818

| 01

01 *The exquisite Brut Réserve*
02 *The family House in Mareuil-sur-Aÿ*

Notre Dame du Gruguet, surrounded by vineyards and looking down across the Vallée de la Marne, we drank a few glasses of 1966 Cuvée Nicolas François and he explained that he was a fastidious operator with minute attention to detail. His wines, he felt, were some of the purest in the region and this purity gave them the ability to age incrementally and gracefully. He put this down to his double 'débourbage' technique - a cold stabilisation prior to fermentation when you allow the solids in the juice to settle and be discarded. Billecart-Salmon adopts two of these disciplines for every tank of grape must – a winemaker working for Billecart trialled it because he had experience in the beer business, where it is widely practised, and it made a huge difference to the final wines. This trick stuck, but because it is labour-intensive, very costly and time consuming at a period of the year when you generally need all of your tanks for fermentation, very few Houses do it. This meticulous attention to detail makes the Billecart wines transcendental in the glass and extremely age-worthy, if you have the willpower to hold on to them that long. François then showed me his immaculate cellars – a work of engineering genius and I was immediately hooked on his work ethic, his openness and his wines.

In a few years' time this eminent Champagne will celebrate its 200th birthday. This incredible company was founded in 1818 by Nicolas François

• I remember meeting François Roland-Billecart for the first time nearly 20 years ago. The first thing he did was to drive up to a hill overlooking his village of Mareuil-sur-Aÿ where he filled me in on the background of his family wine business. From our vantage point of the statue of

Billecart and Elisabeth Salmon – whose names are immortalised these days on two of the vintage cuvées. From their home which is also their winery and office, in Mareuil-sur-Aÿ, their descendents François and Antoine Roland-Billecart now oversee the company under the watchful eye of their father Jean Roland-Billecart.

Tastings at Billecart are not always conducted in the official tasting room. I have tasted most of my wines at the kitchen table. Eschewing eating out at one of the many superb restaurants in the region, François loves to cook while I and his wife Edith listen to rock music (they met at Woodstock!) and drink stunning Champagne. I remember being introduced to the anthemic delights of stadium siren Véronique Sanson played at full volume on one of these evenings. This prompted me to give him a present on our next meeting. Trying to influence his tastes with something suitably British, I proffered the seminal Oasis album '(What's the Story) Morning Glory?' and later heard that he played the seven minute, final track Champagne Supernova on a loop during the harvest on the winery stereo.

This is classic François. He is always on top form, disappearing off through a secret door which connects their house to the cellars, later to return with something utterly amazing or sautéing some stunning fish while belting out a Rolling Stones track. While totally relaxed and immensely funny

out of work, he is incredibly focused on his wines and he never stops micro-fine-tuning anything he can. His winery is as pristine as an operating theatre with recent subterranean additions to the ancient cellars and a new emphasis on barrel fermentation - he is continually tinkering away to try to make the finest wines in the world.

Billecart-Salmon is also in a very good position regarding grape supply. They own 50ha of the 170ha they source from, including Le Clos Saint-Hilaire, their 1ha pure Pinot Noir cuvée. I described the 1996 as the finest young Champagne I have ever tasted. Billecart drinkers are a very loyal

group and the distributors around the world are completely dedicated to the brand. François and Antoine ensure that customer service is paramount and this is perfectly demonstrated by the ultra-low (and sometimes no) dosage magnums which they bottle specially for Alain Passard, the legendary three-Michelin-star chef at Arpège in Paris. This wine, albeit not part of the usual Billecart offering, is jaw-dropping and you have to eat at Arpège to drink it – heaven.

I have been lucky enough to taste virtually every great Billecart release in the last 50 years including the legendary 1959

Nicolas François, which was described as the Champagne of the millennium. Don't be blinded by just the top wines though because the NV Brut Réserve, NV Brut Rosé, NV Grand Cru Blanc de Blancs and NV Demi-Sec must be the finest line-up of non-vintage wines in Champagne, with the rosé being a particular favourite with the glitterati. A new and exceptionally brave NV Brut Sous Bois harnesses the impact that oak barrels can have on a wine and the Extra Brut NV and Vintage pair, following this new vogue for searingly dry wines, are little-known and equally thrilling. It will come as no surprise to learn that the vintage foursome of Grande Cuvée, Elisabeth Salmon Rosé, Nicolas François and the Blanc de Blancs are all phenomenal. These are life-changing wines and they only release them when the vintages are sublime (unlike other Houses) and with decent age already under their belts. Atop the portfolio is Le Clos Saint-Hilaire – if I had to choose just one bottle from Champagne, this is it.

03 The Impressive Billecart-Salmon cellars

04 Antoine, Jean and François Roland-Billecart

05 The Pressoir during harvest

Louis Roederer

"These days the Cristal bottle is one of the strongest statements of style and taste imaginable. Backed up by a knockout flavour that combines elegance and power, it can age gracefully and yields an iconic wine style."

Reims
Champagne
Established 1776

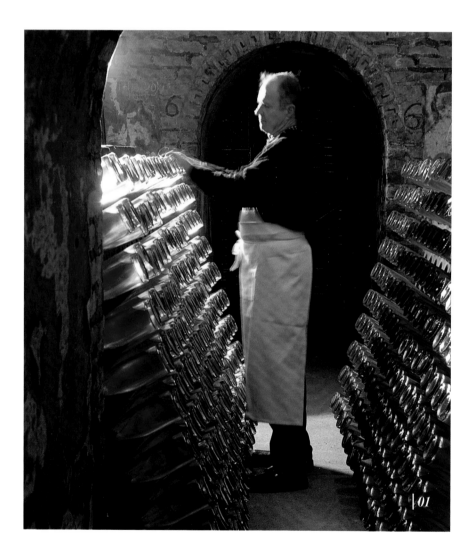

|01

• Louis Roederer was established in 1776. I remember 1976 very well because I was attending an American school, in Brussels, and we celebrated the bicentennial of the Declaration of Independence that year. So, Louis Roederer Champagne is the same age as the United States of America – a fact to certainly make you think.

A family business for well over 200 years, the name Louis Roederer only came into existence in 1833 when Louis himself masterminded the rebranding and growth of this company such that when his son, Louis Roederer II took over, 40 years later, production had reached a staggering 2.5 million bottles – at the time, one tenth of the entire region of Champagne. Back then, well over half a million bottles went to Russia each year and a large amount of wine was shipped to America, too, so over a century and a half ago Roederer basked in a truly global market. Unfortunately with a lot of your eggs in these two particular baskets, the Russian Revolution, US Prohibition and the Stock Market crisis of 1929 all wounded the Champagne House severely. It did however remain in family hands and a slow rebuilding process took place.

In 1979 Jean-Claude Rouzaud took over from his grandmother Camille Olry-Roederer and it was his appointment which provided Louis Roederer with a welcome renaissance. This incredible Champagne House was the very first winery that I ever visited, back in 1987, and it had a profound

effect on me. Jean-Claude showed me around; I tasted the entire range and fell in love with Champagne at that moment. Over 25 years ago the image of Roederer was an enviable one. There was a handcrafted feel to the wines, counterpointed by their slick, polished, business side with its dynamic international contacts.

Nothing has changed today in spite of the fact that production has risen, vineyard holdings have been substantially increased (they own 230ha of vines in all three main regions of Champagne) and Roederer now sits atop a portfolio of smart wineries. That the portfolio, now run by Jean-Claude's son Frédéric, includes a panoply of like-minded, elite, locally-run blue chip estates - Roederer Estate and Scharffenberger, both in California, Champagne Deutz, Maison Delas in the Rhône Valley, Ramos Pinto in the Douro Valley, Portugal, Domaines Ott in Provence, Château de Pez and Château Haut Beauséjour (Saint-Estèphe), Château Pichon-Longueville Comtesse de Lalande (Pauillac) and Château Bernadotte (Haut-

Médoc) all in Bordeaux, is truly staggering. Back to Reims and Roederer, the House which has made one word synonymous with vinous luxury - Cristal.

In the late 1800s Tsar Alexander II wanted to differentiate his Champagne from those bottles which his subjects enjoyed and so his cellar-master asked Louis Roederer to come up with something ingenious. A Flemish glass master designed a clear 'crystal' bottle with a flat bottom and Cristal was born. As the official supplier of Champagne to the Imperial Court of Russia, Roederer suddenly, and perhaps unwittingly, launched one of the marketing coups of the modern wine world. These days the Cristal bottle is one of the strongest statements of style and taste imaginable. Backed up by a knockout flavour that combines elegance and power, it can age gracefully and yields an iconic wine style. The only problem that this wine has is that it is almost always drunk too young. It is put on the market at around eight to 10

years old and this is half what it needs to get into its stride, so please take note.

The rest of the portfolio is important to elaborate on too however, as it does the hard work that allows Cristal to lounge resplendently at the top of the pile. Brut Premier is the name of the non-vintage cuvée at Louis Roederer and it is one of the most reliably excellent wines available. The knack of making memorable non-vintage Champagne is to retain a strong and recognisable House style regardless of what the vagaries of the vintages throw at you.

01 *Each bottle of Cristal is riddled by hand*
02 *A Louis Roederer vineyard*

| 03

You do this by blending across various harvests (usually three), using the three grapes of Champagne, Pinot Noir, Pinot Meunier and Chardonnay, from a multitude of different vineyard sites. In short the permutations and combinations are endless, but Brut Premier always tastes serene, noble and languid.

It doesn't matter how you're feeling – Brut Premier will lift your spirits. Its consistency and delicious flavour make it many peoples' NV of choice. Above Brut Premier, the Vintage Blanc de Blancs is a silky, pure Chardonnay cuvée with even more magical freshness and levity than found in Brut Premier. The two vintage cuvées are sublime – Brut Vintage and Brut Vintage Rosé are not as forceful and intense as many, but it is their subtlety and

length of flavour that wins over so many palates. Partnering Cristal is the ethereal, rare and very expensive Cristal Rosé, first released in 1974, which is regarded by many as the ultimate incarnation of its kind. Finally there is Carte Blanche, a Demi-Sec style of wine which is utterly decadent with fruity puddings. I also adore this wine served ice cold as a retro aperitif.

So rather than thinking of Louis Roederer as a company which hangs its other Champagnes off Cristal's fame, I see it as one which has built its empire on Brut Premier's excellence. I encourage you to strengthen your own foundations with this phenomenal wine, too.

04

05

03 The door that leads into Champagne
    Louis Roederer's famous Reserve
    Cellar. One of the house's great-
    est assets contributing depth to its
    wines

04 An example of how to store Cristal
    in style

05 Cristal moments

Bollinger

"I drink it when I am happy and when I'm sad. Sometimes I drink it when I'm alone. When I have company I consider it obligatory. I trifle with it if I'm not hungry and drink it when I am. Otherwise I never touch it – unless I'm thirsty."

Aÿ
Champagne
Established 1829

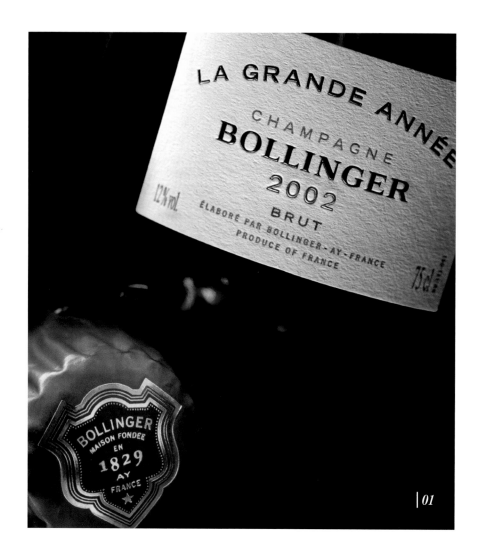

| 01

• Over 50 years ago, the national newspaper for whom I write a weekly column, interviewed one of the most respected women in the wine trade, Madame Lily Bollinger. In London to launch the first vintage of Bollinger RD Champagne (the 1952) she famously said of her beloved Champagne: "I drink it when I am happy and when I'm sad. Sometimes I drink it when I'm alone. When I have company I consider it obligatory. I trifle with it if I'm not hungry and drink it when I am. Otherwise I never touch it – unless I'm thirsty."

This quote stood the test of time and adorns the walls of restaurants and wine bars the world over. Most students of wine learn these words long before they even taste Bollinger Champagne.

The Bollinger story starts over 500 years ago when the Hennequin family settled in Champagne, buying vineyards in Cramant, Cuis and Aÿ. In 1829 the Renaudin, Bollinger & Co. partnership was founded by Anathase de Villermont, his wife, Jacques Bollinger and Paul Renaudin along with the acquisition of top quality vineyards in the locale – a wise custom which continues today. Jacques married Louise Charlotte Hennequin de Villermont and the Bollinger Company was born. When Renaudin-Bollinger set up an office, Bollinger-Mentzendorff, in London over 150 years ago, only 10% of Bollinger's Champagne production was destined for the UK. By

1884 however, Queen Victoria had become such a fan that she granted Bollinger a Royal Warrant and by the time Joseph Jacob died that year, Bollinger's exports to Great Britain had risen to a giddy 89% with a further 7% heading out to the Empire. With Royal Warrants from the Prince of Wales and King Edward VII, Bollinger's fame was unprecedented and Jacques's sons Joseph and Georges took over the reins.

The House was awarded another Royal Warrant from King George V. In 1911 Harry J. Newman, the director of London agents Mentzendorff, created a new brand name for Bollinger – 'Special Cuvée Very Dry', the brand that we all know and love today. Georges' son Jacques took over the company in 1918 and made a superb decision in marrying Elizabeth Law de Lauriston-Boubers, known as 'Lily'. Galvanised by her spirit and support, he further expanded the winery and offices and built new cellars. When he tragically died in 1941, Mme Lily, a childless widow took up the reins alone as the head of the

Bollinger House, at a time when it was unheard of for a woman to hold such a position. Mme Lily led the House through the war including the devastating bombing of Aÿ in August 1944. She was known and loved for her community spirit and tireless work ethic. A keen cyclist, she pedalled all over the region to inspect her vineyards and keep up with her devoted grape growers.

As well as being a local hero, she was also a brand ambassador setting the scene for the image of today's Bollinger. She acquired new vineyards in Aÿ, Mutigny, Grauves and Bisseuil, strengthening Bollinger's supply of top class grapes, resulting in George VI awarding her a fifth Royal Warrant in 1950, and Queen Elizabeth II her sixth in 1955. It was in 1956 that a certain James Bond was seen drinking Bollinger for the first time in Ian Fleming's novel 'Diamonds are Forever' thereby kick-starting an enviable relationship that continues to this day.

In 1961 Lily created the concept of R.D. (Recently Disgorged) Champagne; an

aged, vintage wine kept in the cellar for late release, so the collector could enjoy perfectly mature Champagne mellowed in the very cellar in which it was made. She showed innovation in improving the winemaking and grape growing processes using a rudimentary 'sorting table' to eliminate unripe or rotten grapes after the harvest. In 1968 she was invited to London to preside over the Wine & Spirit Benevolent Society's annual dinner - an all-male preserve.

01 Bollinger La Grande Année 2002
02 Maison Bollinger

Her speech was applauded by 1100 members and she was given a standing ovation. A year later, Lily also created Bollinger's Vieilles Vignes Françaises, from two small, unique plots of ungrafted vines situated next to her house in Aÿ. This is the most coveted Champagne of all and even in retirement she created a new name for the vintage release in 1976 - Grande Année. She also won the Chevalier of the National Order of Merit. In 1971 Lily's nephew Claude d'Hautefeuille took over and continued the modernisation of the estate, acquiring more vineyards. When Lily died in 1977 the wine world was left in deep mourning.

Christian Bizot, Claude's cousin, succeeded shortly after, further developing the brand internationally with 60% of the total grape supply estate-owned - an enviable statistic. Bollinger was the name on everyone's lips while the James Bond link is still thriving nearly 50 years on, with 007 moving neatly from Bollinger's iconic

R.D. to La Grande Année. Charismatic Ghislain de Montgolfier took over as president in 1993 and he remained in charge until 2008 when Jérôme Philipon assumed the role; carefully guiding Bollinger to its position today as one of the most highly respected of all Champagne houses. The dominance of Pinot Noir, Aÿ's Grand Cru grape, in each Bollinger wine is also a crucial factor. The primary fermentation of Bollinger takes place in oak barrels (rare in Champagne) while the extraordinary 'reserve wines' all stored in magnums in the cellars are then blended into the Special Cuvée, lending it unique, distinguished flavour. Over 600,000 magnums of reserve wines are kept in Bollinger's cellars! The elite line-up of cuvées starts with two non-vintage wines - the world famous Special Cuvée and a recently released Rosé, followed by the stunning vintage duo of La Grande Année and La Grande Année Rosé, (another Lily creation) as well as the two vintage wines R.D.('recently disgorged') and the VVF right at the top of the tree.

If you ever visit Bollinger, on a private tour, you may sense the resolve felt by the Count de Villermont, Jacques Bollinger and Madame Lily to honour these vineyards with their unforgettable style of wine. We are all very grateful for their passion and vision.

03   *Bollinger stone marker*
04   *Old oak barrels used for fermentation*
05   *Pinot Noir grapes*

Filliatreau

• Fred and his father Paul run this superb Domaine in Saumur-Champigny. With only a handful of juicy red Cabernet Franc wines on their list you might be wondering how they have made the grade for this book, but I can tell you that these are some of the most thoughtful and uplifting reds I have ever tasted. In weaker vintages they are immediate, jolly and happy-go-lucky, giving you untold pleasure at a snip of the price. In great vintages they mature along the lines of decent Right Bank claret and provide some of the finest value Grand Vin experiences I can think of. Look to the inexpensive Saumur Château Fouquet for instant gratification and then graduate to Saumur-Champigny La Grande Vignolle for intricate violet and graphite notes, before finishing off with the imperial Vieilles Vignes – a mesmerising and peerless glimpse of what Loire Cabernet Franc is capable of.

Huet

• Domaine Huet is the globally acknowledged master of age-worthy Chenin Blanc. An ancient bottle of Vouvray Clos du Bourg could be as fresh as a summer meadow and autumn orchard rolled into one. The great Gaston Huet, who passed away in 2002, inherited this estate from his father Victor and mother Anna-Constance, who bought it in 1929. Until recently the estate was run by Gaston's son-in-law Noël Pinguet and with the security of substantial investment it looks set to cruise into the next generation, with winemaking controlled by local lad Benjamin Joliveau and long time cellar-master Jean-Bernard Berthomé. The 35ha estate includes a set of stunning 'lieu dits' and these make a bewildering array of styles of wines. Sparkling wines, Sec (dry), Demi-Sec and also Moelleux (sweet) styles can come from any of the three exceptional vineyards, Le Haut-Lieu, Clos du Bourg and Le Mont depending on the quality of the vintage. Le Constance, a botrytised cuvée named after Gaston's mother, is also made in exceptional vintages.

Bernard Baudry

"The portfolio of wines at Baudry is easy to understand with a keen opening trio of white, rosé and red to get you salivating."

Chinon
Loire
Established 1975

| 01

• I knew nothing about Bernard Baudry's wines until London wine merchants Haynes, Hanson & Clark poured a few samples for me in order to try to coax me into buying them for Bibendum Restaurant – a wine list I have compiled since 1990. I have always been a fan of Loire wines, not least because the finest Domaines offer world-class flavours, and for some inexplicable reason they still manage to offer incredible value for money. Chinon is one of the great names of which the reds, made from Cabernet Franc and the rarer whites, made from Chenin Blanc capture the wild essence and fascination of the region. Well-chosen versions can seriously shock and impress.

I was ready to be wowed by Baudry's wines, but nothing prepared me for the flavours that I encountered. Without a doubt, the finest red and white wines I have ever tasted from Chinon are produced at this Domaine. They are now a permanent fixture on Bibendum's wine list, as well as in my cellar.

Bernard studied oenology in Beaune and then went to work as a wine consultant in a laboratory in Tours – not far from his final settling place in the Touraine stronghold of Chinon. He started his operation in 1975 with a tiny 2ha, but this has grown to 30ha today and his son Matthieu now runs the Domaine himself, having joined his father in 2000. With experience making wine in Burgundy, Bordeaux, Tasmania and also

California under his belt, he is a highly talented chap. I can't help but think that international experience always pushes estates to the next level.

The portfolio of wines at Baudry is easy to understand with a keen opening trio of white, rosé and red to get you salivating. Each of these wines acts as the definition of the style. They are detailed, accurate, exciting and clearly the work of a craftsman, but with this trio acting as the first rungs on the ladder, you will have already guessed that there is more to discover as you climb. Starting with the other reds, Les Granges comes from a single 6ha 'lieu dit' in Baudry's home village of Cravant-les-Côteaux. This is an expressive, aromatic Cabernet Franc, with the violet and blackberry notes that makes this grape such a sensational, aromatic proposition. There is a levity and briskness to the finish which encourages you to glug it, not something that happens with many wines in this book! The next red is Les Grézeaux; this time with more obvious gravel and stones in

the soil and the oldest plots of vines in the estate. It is an age-worthy wine but one that doesn't seem too tannic in its youth. The use of older oak - as often happens with the most sensitive winemakers in this book - is spot on, making this a savoury and lip-smacking wine with a stunning purple hue and a mass of hedgerow fruit on the palate. Le Clos Guillot is the next Chinon; this time with a more polished feel and a more obvious texture. A suave, layered Cabernet Franc with a magical touch and summer pudding flavours, this is a wine full of élan.

All of these wines drink well in their youth, but also age remarkably well. La Croix Boissée is the most backward of the bunch and it is also the top Cabernet Franc made at this estate. Made from a sublime plot of south-facing vines, this is the richest and most structured of the wines and it is the only one that sees a smidgen of new oak. Only small quantities are made and this is one of the most profound Cabernet Francs I have ever tasted. Served blind it's one of the most difficult wines for people

to pin down, not least because they rarely put Loire in the frame when trying to decide upon a region for a serious red - which is crazy, as this magnificent wine shows.

There is one other wine in the cellars at Baudry which I absolutely adore. It is the white sibling to the red La Croix Boissée and it is a wine of rare beauty. Coming from only 1ha of Chenin Blanc vines, this wine rivals top-flight Chardonnay and yet with its Chenin range of fruit tones there is a touch of exoticism under the stunning nutmeg and patisserie-kissed chassis. It is one of the hidden gems of the wine world and it further cements Baudry's reputation as one of the most important winemakers in the world.

01 *Bernard Baudry's sign*
02 *30ha of vineyards planted on various types of soils*

Jacky&Jean-Philippe Blot de la Taille aux Loups

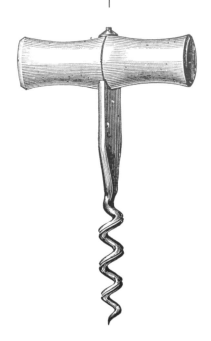

• With an extraordinary work ethic including two sets of grape sorting, at picking and then again on tables in the vineyard before the fruit even makes it to the winery, this father and son team make the most crystalline and pure Chenin Blancs in the Valley. From a superb sparkling Triple Zero, with no added sugar whatsoever, to two of the most beautiful Montlouis Secs I have ever tasted – the taut, mineral-like Les Dix Arpents and the broad, sweepingly regal, mildly oaked Rémus - these are vital and nerve-tingling wines. A gripping Vouvray Sec Clos de la Bretonnière leads on to a phenomenal, kaleidoscopic Montlouis Moelleux Cuvée des Loups. This is a seriously professional Domaine, aiming to bring the wines of this largely forgotten appellation to a global audience. With bottling like this they cannot fail to live up to their wildest of dreams.

François Cotat

• François Cotat makes the most extraordinary and unconventional wines in the world-famous region of Sancerre. With some incredible vineyards in the hamlet of Chavignol, namely Les Culs de Beaujeu, Les Monts Damnés and La Grande Côte, he makes the Sauvignon Blanc grape taste unlike anything else in the world. Late-picking and use of oak are two unusual practices which he adopts, and this seems to focus the flavours and add richness at the same time as dragging chalky and stony minerality from his precipitous vineyards. He also makes wines that age, which is never usually an option for this oft ephemeral variety. I have drunk Cotat wines of 15 and even 20 years of age and they are sensational. The richness of fruit with touches of greengage, talc, lime zest and nut oil is incredible. Every region needs a maverick, but they are never normally the ones who make the best wines.

Marcel Deiss

"The pheremonal pleasure in drinking Deiss wines is simply thrilling and you will not believe what your taste buds are telling you!"

Bergheim
Alsace
Established 1744

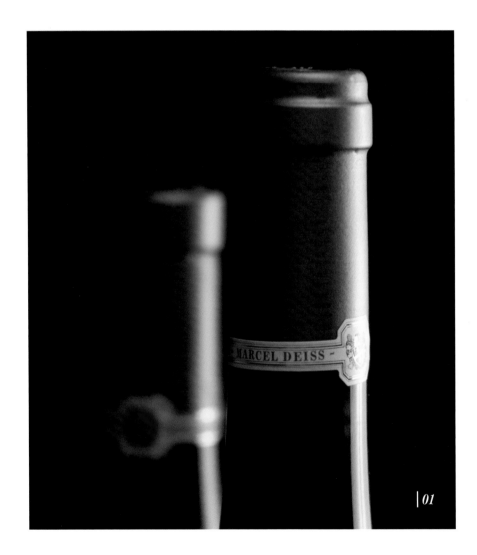

| 01

• While I would love to be able to say that I drink wines from the pages of this book every day, the reality is that I sadly don't quite manage this Elysian pleasure. Of all of the estates in my 100, I probably taste Marcel Deiss' wines the least, but this only heightens the excitement when I do because they are made in tiny quantities and are extremely rare. Thankfully they are not too dear, so you have no excuse not to wade in when you track some bottles down. Domaine Marcel Deiss is located in Bergheim, a small village situated right in the centre of the Alsace region in Northern France. Jean-Michel Deiss is the current winemaker in a long line of vinous alchemists dating back to 1744.

Jean-Michel's estate is spread throughout the region, covering 26ha of prime hillside vineyards in nine different communes. His philosophy is to capture the essence of each of these terroirs in his wines and for that reason his is a follower of biodynamics, like so many of the other esteemed estates in this book. He seeks to match the grape variety exactly to the soil and then bring out the best in both via the conditions of each different vintage. This obsession with each distinct plot of land, the complex geological details of the soils, and then the hand-tending required to coax the finest work from his vines, has led Jean-Michel to classify his own wines in three categories. His Vins de Fruits are varietally labelled wines from a single designated commune or village. These are the easiest to understand because they follow the norm in the region.

The second category is more abstract and it has made him somewhat of an outspoken maverick among his peers. The Vins de Terroirs are field blends of different grape varieties which are linked by their distinct terroir, site and soil. So unlike virtually every other winemaker in the region, Jean-Michel has lots of different varieties planted in each of his 'Premier Cru' and Grand Cru sites which all go into the wines. This intentional muddling of flavours is, in theory, supposed to bring out the true characteristics of the soil rather than one single tone, which is what he suggests happens when you plant only one variety. The last group is the Vins de Temps, which are all classic, late-harvested wines following the Vendange Tardive and Sélection de Grains Nobles guidelines.

This all adds up to a fascinating and incredibly diverse portfolio of wines. It may seem odd to read his labels which declare the name of a Grand Cru vineyard without an accompanying single grape variety, and indeed this was declared illegal by the Institut National des Appellations d'Origine, but this decision was reversed in 2005 to allow Deiss to thankfully do what he likes. Deiss' decision to stick to his guns has won him many admirers. You can buy his Vins de Fruits wines, as I do, and bathe in the purity and laser-driven expression of each and every single varietal, but it is the Vins de Terroirs wines that blow the mind, confounding your taste buds. Look out for the spectacular Grand Cru Schoenenbourg which was planted in the 1930s with Pinot Gris, Muscat, Riesling Gewurztraminer and Sylvaner.

This wine conjures up the musk, grass, bark, zest, kernel and root notes of the finest perfumers. His Grand Cru Altenberg de Bergheim is a tour de force, too.

Usually an exclusively Gewurztraminer-based wine in other hands, Deiss weaves mainly Riesling and all 13 grape varieties used in Alsace, creating an otherworldly joy that is incomparable to any other wine.

His so-called 'Premier Cru' Englegarten uses Pinot Blanc, Pinot Gris, Riesling and Muscat to devastating effect, too. The pheremonal pleasure in drinking Deiss wines is simply thrilling and you will not believe what your taste buds are telling you!

01   Marcel Deiss neck label
02   Grand Cru Mambourg vines

| 02

Kaysersberg
Alsace

Weinbach

• Weinbach is one of my 'desert island' producers. Meaning 'wine brook', it has been planted to vines since 890 and it was officially established by Capuchin monks in 1612. Nowadays it is run by the powerful triumvirate of Colette, Catherine and Laurence Faller and they make some of the most beautiful Gewurztraminer, Riesling and Pinot Gris in existence. The portfolio is serious and the wines range from lush, dry, enigmatic creations to unimaginably exotic, mesmerising sweet wines. The glamorous Catherine Faller always pours liquid gold into my glass when I taste with her. I am totally enamoured by the Riesling Schlossberg Cuvée Ste. Catherine, Gewurztraminer Furstentum, Pinot Gris Altenbourg Cuvée d'Or Quintessence (which I have awarded a perfect 20/20 to) and the delectable Riesling Altenbourg Vendanges Tardive.

Domaine François Raveneau

- The Domaine was established in 1948 by its namesake and today, François' sons, Bernard and Jean-Marie, run the vineyards and winemaking in exactly the same manner as their father and the results are spectacular. With 8ha of vines including six superb Premier Crus - Montée de Tonnerre, Butteaux, Forêt, Vaillons, Monts Mains and Chapelot and three mind-blowing Grand Crus - Valmur, Blanchot and Clos, this is a very serious operation indeed. Sadly, François passed away in 2000, but his memory lives on and his legacy is very easy to encapsulate in one sentence. His wines are the greatest true expressions of Chablis I have ever tasted.

Domaine Ramonet

• The most famous winemakers in the picturesque village of Chassagne-Montrachet are the Ramonets. André Ramonet has passed on his business to his two sons, Noël and Jean-Claude. With three Grands Crus - Montrachet, Bâtard-Montrachet and Bienvenue Bâtard-Montrachet; a flight of Chassagne Premiers Crus including Champs-Canet, Les Caillerets, Les Ruchottes, Boudriotte, Morgeot, Les Vergers and Les Chaumées, (not forgetting a village level Chassagne-Montrachet that equals many other estates' 1er Crus) this talented clan is sitting on a goldmine. They make wines with incredible definition and sense of place added to the fact that they age exceptionally well, too. With 34ha under vine it is important to note that half of this is red, and thanks to the popularity of the whites, the reds are uncommon value for money. Keep your eyes peeled for 1er Crus Clos de la Boudriotte and Clos Saint-Jean – they are gorgeously fragrant Pinots to drink after you have polished off a few of the majestic Chardonnays.

Etienne Sauzet

• Gérard Boudot, his daughter Emilie and her husband Benoît Riffault run this fantastic estate looking directly at the Côte d'Or from their winery door. Gérard augments his own vineyards by buying parcels of fruit from top flight growers and his portfolio represents the greatest hits of his beloved village of Puligny. With Montrachet, Chevalier-Montrachet, Bâtard-Montrachet and Bienvenues-Bâtard-Montrachet, all Grands Crus and Puligny-Montrachet Premiers Crus Les Combettes, Champ Gain, Les Folatières, Champ Canet, La Garenne, Les Perrières, Les Referts, Hameau de Blagny, Village Puligny-Montrachet and Chassagne-Montrachet, you would be churlish not to track down a bottle and experience the sheer beauty and magnetic attraction of his creations. With a biodynamic regime in full swing I expect even more finesse in these wines, if that is indeed possible. If you cannot find one of these star wines then his Sauzet Bourgogne Blanc is an eminently affordable sneak preview of Gérard's genius at an everyday price – keep this advice under your beret!

Domaine des Comtes Lafon

• By contrast to Coche-Dury's taut, linear wines, the Comtes Lafon's Meursaults are positively exotic and decorously upholstered. They have the most amazing sumptuous fruit and it makes them desperately attractive even in their youth. With both red and white wines at this Domaine, Dominique Lafon has cracked both codes at the highest level – something other estates struggle to achieve. His Volnays are sublime with stunning, intense black cherry fruit and epic, spicy oak. His late-harvested, low-yielding Meursault vines make unbelievably sensual cuvées. From a stunning Village, via the incredible Clos de la Barre monopole behind the house and the delicate 'lieu dit' Désirée, to no less than six epic Meursault Premiers Crus - Charmes, Goutte d'Or, Porusots, Bouchères, Genevrières and Perrières. The Grand Cru Montrachet completes the picture and you won't be surprised to hear that there are several candidates in this list who've been awarded a perfect 20/20 in my notes.

Domaine Leflaive

"These Chardonnays have come to be recognised as the finest expressions of this variety on the planet."

Puligny-Montrachet
Burgundy
Established 1717

• There is a 2000-year vine-growing history in Puligny. It is thought that this quaint, sleepy village, nestling in the Côte de Beaune, and home to the greatest Chardonnay vines in the world, derives its name from a pioneering Roman called Puliniacus who picked the finest spot on earth to cultivate vines. The Leflaive history dates back to 1717, as the labels proudly state. It was Claude Leflaive who built his house on the square in the middle of the village, nearly 300 years ago, and 10 generations of Leflaives have lived there ever since. Joseph Leflaive, formally an engineer who designed France's first submarine, revitalised and expanded the estate in 1920, after the phylloxera epidemic had done its damage and land prices hit an all-time low.

He and his estate manager François Virot replanted the vines on roots which were resistant to this louse, and this marked the beginning of wines sold under the Leflaive name. After Joseph's death in 1953, his four children took over the running of the estate with Jo (Joseph) handling the administration and finance and Vincent looking after the vineyards, winemaking and brand-building.

Over the next 40 years their combined passion and skill brought Leflaive's wines to a worldwide audience. These Chardonnays have come to be recognised as the finest expressions of this variety on the planet. In 1990 Anne-Claude Leflaive, Vincent's daughter, took over the management of

the company, supported by a strong family group and she remains there to this day. I first toured Burgundy in 1992 and I was more excited about visiting Domaine Leflaive than any other producer. I travelled with Philip Bailey, the wine buyer for Green's Restaurant and Oyster Bar in St. James's, in London, and he was as nervous as I was as we pulled into the courtyard of the beautiful Domaine in the centre of the village. As we got out of the car, a mighty figure walked out of the front door and stood at the top of the steps looking down on us. I was just about to splutter my finest French greetings when he beat me to it saying, 'Hello dear boy', in possibly the poshest English accent I had ever heard. This was, of course, the great Vincent Leflaive and for the next hour we were completely enraptured by one of the most renowned gentlemen in the history of the wine world. I will never forget his ribald sense of humour and perfect command of English. His one rule in the cellar was, 'ne pas cracher parterre', which he said winking and gesticulating towards the

ornate spittoon/fountain device on the wall, and it has stuck in my mind since that day.

When you are invited to taste at grand estates in Burgundy, never assume that you will taste 'toute la gamme' - all of the range. This often means that Grand Cru wines are not mentioned and you are politely shown the door, after debating the various Premiers Crus. This didn't happen at Leflaive. Vincent poured samples of every single one of his wines including the minuscule production Montrachet. He was generous to a fault and I have never forgotten his warmth and his willingness to explain all that he could about his wines and his vineyards. As I drove away I realised that I had just tasted at the greatest white wine estate in the world.

The following year Vincent Leflaive passed away and I felt extraordinarily emotional about this, but incredibly privileged to have met him. I visit the Domaine regularly and Anne-Claude has followed in her father's footsteps. She has, in my opinion, taken

the wines of Leflaive to new heights. From the early '90s they worked their vineyards biodynamically and gained certification in 1997. This has brought a new and vibrant dimension to these profound, enigmatic wines. During one visit, Anne-Claude noticed that I had shortened the name of her Bourgogne Blanc to BBBB in my notebook. She asked why and I told her that when I had asked her on a previous visit where the Bourgogne Blanc vineyards were she had replied 'derrière le bâtiment' or behind the building. In my haste I had noted down Bourgogne Blanc Behind Bâtiment and it had stuck – after all, most white wines producers in Burgundy make a Bourgogne Blanc, and it seemed fitting that there was only one BBBB. She rather liked this little story and apparently refers to her wine like this on occasion!

01   *The famous label*
02   *Domaine Leflaive*

Leflaive wines are all celestial, precise interpretations of their exact vineyard locations. They are made with the utmost care and the results are nothing short of life-changing. With no less than four Grands Crus-Montrachet (a tiny parcel of 0.08 ha), Chevalier-Montrachet (three parcels of just under 2ha), Bienvenues-Bâtard-Montrachet (one parcel of 1.1ha) and Bâtard-Montrachet (four parcels of just under 2 ha) this is the ultimate portfolio of imperial Chardonnay real estate. The four excellent Puligny-Montrachet Premier Crus include Les Pucelles, Les Folatières, Les Combettes and Le Clavoillon with a Meursault Premier Cru, sous le Dos d'Âne, to complete this level. The 'village' Puligny-Montrachet is made from seven parcels across the hillside totalling 4.6ha – so you should, at the very least, be able to track some of this down! The final wine is the aforementioned BBBB which comes from two plots, you know where, and it is a wine that I buy every single year for its élan and tremendous value.

| 03

| 04

03   *Anne-Claude Leflaive*
04   *The horse-ploughed vineyards*
05   *The courtyard at Domaine Leflaive*

Domaine Jean-François Coche-Dury

• The key to the wines of Coche-Dury is that they are picked relatively early, which preserves high acidity in the grapes and results in raspingly fresh Chardonnay flavours. Because acidity is the life blood of white wines, Coche-Dury's Meursaults age unlike any other white wines in the Côte de Beaune. Open a 10-year-old Bourgogne Blanc (the lowest rung on the ladder, albeit a Coche BB, so still a very dear wine) and it will burst out of the glass with vivacity and zing. The most famous and expensive wine in the range is the Grand Cru Corton-Charlemagne but it is the range of Meursaults that I hunt down. Premiers Crus Perrières, Caillerets and Genévrières are off the scale and two 'lieu dits' Meursault Les Chevalières and Les Rougeots are also staggeringly serious. J-F's son Raphaël Coche has taken over from his legendary father and the wines continue to thrill everyone who tastes them.

Domaine Bonneau du Martray

• Jean-Charles le Bault de la Morinière took over from his father Jean in 1994 after giving up his career as an architect. He has taken this estate a long way in nearly two decades and the wines are finer and more attractive than ever. He also is edging towards a biodynamic regime in the vineyards which has certainly made a difference to both the Corton-Charlemagne Grand Cru and its red brother Corton Grand Cru. The 11 ha of vines, all on the Pernand side of the magnificent Corton hill, are split up into many different parcels and they are vinified separately before being carefully reassembled to make the finished wine. I am a massive fan of the Corton-Charlemagne from this property not least because it is a shimmering beauty, and also because it is my wife Amelia's favourite white wine!

Domaine G. Roumier

• Christophe Roumier makes wonderfully sensual, aromatically exact wines from his base in Chambolle and he brings us one of the most heavenly-scented Pinots imaginable, in the form of the romantically entitled Chambolle-Musigny, 1er Cru Les Amoureuses. He makes 1er Cru Les Cras and the more structured duo Bonnes-Mares and Musigny Grand Cru from his own village. He also sources fruit from neighbouring Morey-St-Denis where he makes a delightfully chewy, succulent 1er Cru Clos de la Bussière as well as over the village border into Gevrey, where he owns a tiny slice of Grand Cru Charmes-Chambertin. All of his wines are ethereally proportioned; utterly seductive and charming in their youth and they age like clockwork, too.

Chambolle-Musigny
Burgundy

Domaine Comte Georges de Vogüé

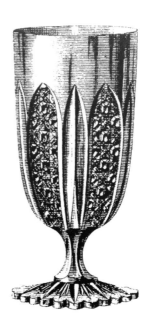

● With over 500 years of history this Domaine is one of the mighty names of Burgundy with a very small portfolio of elite wines from some of the most famous plots of wine in the region. Based in the stunning village of Chambolle-Musigny, de Vogüé is most famous for its Grand Cru Musigny Cuvée Vieilles Vignes, one of the longest lived Pinot Noirs in the world. Another Grand Cru, Bonnes-Mares, also packs a stunning punch but the most elegant and succulent Pinot is the heavenly Chambolle 1er Cru, Les Amoureuses. Made from a tiny parcel of fruit, this is often my favourite wine in the estate on account of its texture and heady earthiness. Only the old vines go into the Musigny, so any wines younger than 25 years old in this Grand Cru vineyard are declassified for a Chambolle-Musigny Premier Cru - remarkable value in the greater scheme of things.

Domaine Méo-Camuzet

• At the beginning of the 20th century, Etienne Camuzet sought out impeccable parcels of land for his fledgling wine business. Etienne's daughter Maria Noirot bequeathed the estate to a distant relative Jean Méo who continued in his job in Paris and let out some of the vineyards to support the winery. These days, his son Jean-Nicolas Méo runs the business and some of the vineyards are still leased, with the majority now being used for the Domaine's own incredible wines. The godfather of modern red winemaking, Henri Jayer was a consultant to the property, which set it out on a great footing. Today the wines are as fine as any on the Côte and with extraordinary holdings including my favourites - Grands Crus Richebourg, Clos de Vougeot, Corton Clos Rognet, Premiers Crus Vosne-Romanée Aux Brûlées, Vosne-Romanée Au Cros Parantoux, Vosne-Romanée Les Chaumes, Nuits-Saint-Georges Aux Boudots, Nuits-Saint-Georges Aux Murgers and two amazing Village level wines - Nuits-Saint-Georges and Vosne-Romanée, this estate is flying very high indeed. They have recently added a 'négociant' arm under the Méo-Camuzet Frère & Sœurs label.

Domaine Ponsot

• Laurent Ponsot is one of the nicest men in Burgundy and tasting at his winery in Morey is a sheer pleasure. With a diverse portfolio of a handful of Village wines, several stunning Premiers Crus and a massive 10 Grands Crus which all express their exact origins, it is the perfect place to get an overview of any particular vintage. My picks from his amazing range include the white Morey-Saint-Denis, 1er Cru Clos des Monts Luisants made from 100-year-old Aligoté vines which is truly mesmerising. In the reds I adore the Chambolle-Musigny 1er Cru Charmes, the Grand Cru Clos Saint Denis Cuvée Très Vieilles Vignes made from over 100-year-old vines, and the Clos de la Roche Cuvée Vieilles Vignes - one of the most impactful and important wines in the Côte de Nuits. He also has a Griotte Chambertin and Chambertin that are mind-blowing. This is an unmissable Domaine.

Domaine de la Romanée Conti

"It is the exact positioning of these hallowed vineyards which is responsible for making the flavours and the longevity of these wines the most sought-after and most expensive on the planet."

Vosne-Romanée
Burgundy
Established 13th Century

| 01

• I am often asked what my favourite estate is in the world. I have also been asked what the number one estate in this book is. It is impossible to decide on a favourite estate because they are all so different and there is no number one in this book – because by virtue of their inclusion they are all number ones. But an easier question to answer is - if you had one bottle of wine to drink for dinner this evening, what would it be? My reply would be La Tâche, DRC and I suspect that I would need a very large table and a lot of bottles because it would be the answer of many of us who have tasted the wines from this venerable estate.

Domaine de la Romanée-Conti, virtually always shortened to DRC in conversation, wears the crown in Burgundy. It is, without doubt, the most famous Pinot Noir producer in the world. I remember moderating a Pinot Noir symposium in Mornington Peninsula some years ago and Aubert de Villaine, co-owner, with the Leroy family, and director, of DRC was one of the guest speakers. We conducted the largest (I am not sure if this record has been broken) horizontal tasting of DRC wines ever held, too. The tickets for this event literally sold out in seconds. Aubert and his wines cast such a spell over the world it is hard to put into words. I have tasted and drunk DRC wines on many occasions, I am pleased to report, and every single sip has given me goosebumps and moved me in ways that no other wine can.

Originally owned by the Abbey of Saint Vivant, in the 13th century, a prime collection of vineyards in the centre of the village of Vosne passed through several sets of hands before being seized during the French Revolution and sold off. Even Madame de Pompadour, mistress of Louis XV of France, fought for the estate with her bitter enemy Louis François de Bourbon, Prince de Conti and with Conti winning this spat the property became known as Romanée-Conti. Over time and with various different owners, the property grew in size, via a series of very shrewd negotiations, to encompass the finest collection of Grand Cru vineyards ever assembled, including Echézeaux, Grands Echézeaux, Romanée-St-Vivant, Richebourg, the monopole of La Tâche, another of Romanée-Conti and also a plot in the white Grand Cru Montrachet, in the Côte de Beaune. The vine are averages around the 50-year mark and the yields are extremely low (around the 25 hl/ha mark) and with the biodynamic regime that they follow and ploughing using horses, not tractors, all of the signs are here in order to make great wine. But if this was the case, all Grands Crus up and down the Côte de Nuits could perform at this stratospheric level and they do not.

It is the exact positioning of these hallowed vineyards which is responsible for making the flavours and the longevity of these wines the most sought-after and most expensive on the planet. Tasting at DRC is a joy unlike no other. The cellars are ancient, with parts dating back to the previous monastic owners and it is initially staggering to see all of the barrels and bottles of DRC in one place at one time. Usually a rare sighting of a single bottle in a restaurant or wine shop is enough to raise the adrenalin levels to a peak, so when Aubert and his cellarmaster Bernard Noblet then proceed to pipette tasting samples of their wines for you in situ, it is overwhelming. The sheer intensity of power and grace in every one of their wines is staggering. De Villaine's reverence is offset sometimes with Noblet's cheekiness and this lightens the mood

allowing you to remember to breathe. At the end of the tasting we retire to a cavern where Noblet opens a few blind wines and I summon up all of my skills to guess them correctly.

With a fixed number of possible options you might think this challenge is relatively easy, but such is the slow rate of maturation of these regal wines I have, in the past, been two decades out! There are certainly DRC hallmarks which point to each individual Grand Cru, and everyone has their own favourite, but unless you are on a mission to drink a specific wine from a specific vintage, every single opportunity

to taste a bottle should be seized with both hands. With 20ha of awesome vines and a production of around 7500 cases of Grand Cru red wine and only 200 of Montrachet you should, in theory, be able to track down a bottle or two. Be prepared to sell your car though – after all DRC makes do with horses!

01   *The iconic Romanée Conti*
02   *The unique DRC neck label*

| 02

Domaine Armand Rousseau

• One of the greatest meetings and tastings that I have ever experienced was an hour or so spent with the legendary Charles Rousseau, son of the founder Armand. He kindly told me fascinating old stories about the Domaine and its history including the pioneering work they did bottling their own wines back in the 30s. The incredible fact about this amazing estate is that it makes one Gevrey-Chambertin village, one Gevrey-Chambertin Premier Cru - which is a blend - and one which is arguably one of the greatest reds on the planet, Premier Cru Clos Saint Jacques. The other six wines are all Grands Crus - Charmes-Chambertin, Mazy-Chambertin, Clos de la Roche, Ruchottes Chambertin Clos des Ruchottes, Chambertin and Chambertin Clos de Bèze. These are all magnificent and historic creations. Eric Rousseau, Charles' son, is now winemaker and the Rousseau style of laid-back, languid flavours with immense length and 'typicité' continues uninterrupted.

Domaine René & Vincent Dauvissat

• The only rival to Raveneau's crown in Chablis is the impeccable set up at R & V Dauvissat. With over 25 vintages under his belt, Vincent manages 11ha of pristine vineyards including two Grands Crus - Les Clos and Les Preuses, and three Premiers Crus - Vaillons, Séchet and La Forest. A shy, modest man with innate knowledge of his craft, Vincent's wines are the antitheses of the broad, modern, oaky wines from other producers in the region. He prefers to harness the unique minerals and elemental power in his soils and reflect them in his lean, high tensile, starkly stunning creations. Needing a minimum of five years to blossom and living for two decades with ease, these are passionately and intricately assembled wines designed to be drunk by lifelong fans of authentic, reverential winemaking.

Château Thivin

• In 1877 Zaccharie Geoffray bought Château Thivin, and his family has run the property ever since. My only Beaujolais producer in this book is one of the greatest 'vignerons' in France and yet the wines are some of the best value you will ever find. Sensational wines from the Gamay variety; they capture the essence of their village, the history of the region and the drama of top flight Cru Beaujolais. The entry level Côte de Brouilly, Les Sept Vignes, made from a blend of their seven different parcels of vines is sensational. With wild, red berry fruit and a dusting of earthiness and gaminess, this is one of the most thirst-quenching and yet classy wines I have tasted. Seek out the single vineyard cuvées Clos Bertrand and La Chapelle – they age well and are 'Premier' Cru quality. The estate's 'Grand Cru' is called Cuvée Zaccharie, as you might expect.

Château Léoville-Las Cases

• Classified as a Second Growth in the 1855 Classification, Las Cases would certainly graduate to First Growth status if a re-classification ever took place, such is the exceptional quality of the wines made here. Always in the top handful of Châteaux in the Left Bank and more often than not the apogee of the St-Julien commune, the sheer bravado and dark fruit flavours in this wine are a wonder to behold. Some of the finest wines I have ever tasted have come from Léoville-Las Cases, and this is down to the superb vineyards, incredible discipline shown by the winemaker and the steely determination of owner Jean Hubert Delon. The style is opulent, powerful and often tannic and unyielding in its youth, blossoming after 15 or so years into wines that are monumental masterpieces.

1er Cru
Pauillac
Bordeaux

Château Lafite Rothschild

• Lafite is the least opulent and most introverted of the First Growths in its youth. It is a wine that appeals to purists and vinous academics thanks to its compelling, erudite flavours and control on the palate. There is nothing overt or hedonistic about Lafite; preferring to infiltrate your sense by stealth and guile rather than by force. You are immediately calmed with Lafite in your glass and it is the grandeur and restraint which makes this eminent red wine so irresistible. The Cabernet Sauvignon grape shows its elegance and persistence at Lafite more so than at any other Château. It is this character, coupled with its exceptional aging characteristics, which has, no doubt, endeared it to the hearts of the world's most discerning collectors.

Château Pontet-Canet

"Alfred is one of the most elegant gentlemen I have ever had the pleasure of meeting and these wines are made in his image."

5ème Cru
Pauillac
Bordeaux
Established early 18th century

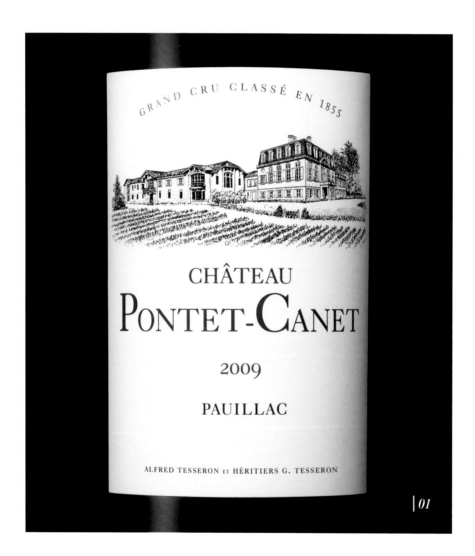

| 01

• While many of the greatest properties in Bordeaux are owned by multinational companies and it is difficult to feel connected to or passionate about the wines or the entities that run them, Pontet-Canet is the diametric opposite. The incredible property is owned by the thoroughly engaging, sage-like Alfred Tesseron. You may be surprised to hear that classed growth Châteaux in Bordeaux can draw fruit from any plot of land that they own in their commune (in this case Pauillac). By contrast, Pontet-Canet's vines are all visible from the vat room (which doubles as a tasting room) in the chai.

This introduces another fascinating fact about this property. A decade ago Alfred Tesseron decided to adopt a strict organic and biodynamic regime at the Château - farming using natural treatments administered in harmony with the phases of the moon. Very few people have adopted these labour-intensive and costly methods of farming in Bordeaux – which is surprising in one of the largest wine regions in the world.

Why has no one else taken the plunge? Perhaps the dramatic, initial drop in yields which come about when you start this new life for the vineyard is one reason. After all, man-made fertilisers and insecticides are designed to promote vine vigour and production, not reduce it. Chemical viticulture tends to stifle a degree of complexity in the wines and they often seem to lack a certain 'je ne sais quoi', compared to wines made from organically grown grapes. Bordeaux is all about money and yet Alfred acknowledged that he would drastically reduce his production and income while the transitional 'shocks' to the vines took place. Considering the increased price of his recent releases, he ought to have more than made up for the initial lower volumes of his crops by now. Also the vines 'recover', never returning to where they were before, but certainly to healthy levels of top class fruit. Having said this, it is still a massive gamble which is all based on the vine itself taking the responsibility for its own balance with the sun, moon, earth and air; all aided gently by the loving viticulturalists and those non-impactful gentle horse hooves.

That Pontet-Canet's deep, intense, multi-faceted flavours have been augmented beyond belief since the 2004 vintage, (when I spotted the changes really impacting on the finished wine) is also a very welcome by-product of this wholly responsible and admirable regime. With an overhauled winery and stunning barrel-room, this Château has rapidly earned super-star status. If I was ever given the pleasure of re-classifying the 1855 Bordeaux 'League Table' Pontet-Canet would rise from 5th Growth to 1st in the blink of an eye. The 2005, 2009 and 2010 vintages of this wine are phenomenal and the difficult 2011 vintage proved Tesseron's belief that a biodynamic vineyard, at total harmony with its terroir and surroundings, can cope with unexpected climatic difficulties, and still yield stunning raw materials. 2011 Pontet-Canet is even more profound than the sublime 2008 vintage; something that speaks volumes for this estate.

So what is this noble land's history and who is Alfred Tesseron? His family is only the third to own this estate since records began in the early 18th century. Alfred's father, Guy, a very famous Cognac shipper, bought the property in 1975 from the Cruse family, who had owned it for 110 years. Pontet-Canet was one of the Château included in the famous 1855 classification. I am lucky enough to have tasted a handful of pre-Tesseron vintages of this wine, including the famous 1961, and there is no doubt that Pontet-Canet's wines were of the very top grade even back then. Today, Pontet-Canet is run by Alfred Tesseron, Guy's son, with his niece Melanie. Spectacularly situated, just south (literally over the road) of the First Growth Châteaux Mouton Rothschild, Pontet-Canet is on a majestic tract of land. In the 81ha of vineyards, Cabernet Sauvignon is king and is augmented with Cabernet Franc, Merlot and a touch of Petit Verdot. The wines are sheer heaven with inky black colour, hedonistic nose and ethereal, intense, immensely long finish.

01 *Château Pontet-Canet 2009*
02 *A horse working the vineyard*

With so much effort going into the tending of the vines and the development of the berries, harvest is kid-glove gentle at Pontet-Canet, with grapes picked into small crates to eliminate bruising or crushing. After this, a forensic sorting procedure (including vibrating tables) takes place; keeping each grape variety and plot separate, ensuring that the precision winemaking gets off to a perfect start. With 90 workers picking and 30 sorting, this is an incredibly finely orchestrated moment in the wine's life and it's exactly what the grapes deserve after the farming element has been so thoughtfully administered. In 2005 Alfred built a stunning modern vat room to augment the traditional oak one and it houses massive, 80 hectolitre re-enforced concrete, truncated cone-shaped vats. These are the ultimate vessels for fermentation because the thermal inertia properties of concrete ensure that the wine's temperature only changes very slowly and gradually enabling the wine to gently retain all of its elemental power and grace. With never more than 60% new oak barrels, Pontet-Canet is all about putting the purity and grace of the fruit first and this is achieved in style. I cannot recommend this and the second wine, Hauts de Pontet-Canet, enough. Alfred is one of the most elegant gentlemen I have ever had the pleasure of meeting and these wines are made in his image.

03 *The Château's new concrete vats*

04 *Alfred and Guy Tesseron with Alfred's niece, Melanie*

05 *Château Pontet-Canet*

Château Latour

"The skill of the winemaker, the endless hours in the vineyards nurturing the vines, the divine setting with its perfect soil and aspect and the ruthlessness of the owner or manager to de-classify sub-standard fruit makes Latour a paragon of perfection."

1er Cru
Pauillac
Bordeaux
Established 1331

| 01

• In April 2012, just after the annual, barrel-sample preview tastings of all of last season's wines, Château Latour issued a missive saying that from this year onwards it would not sell its wines as part of the time-honoured 'en primeur' system and that it would release the wines when they were ready to drink. Frédéric Engerer, the dynamic 'président' of arguably the most important Château in the region, must have taken the utmost pleasure in turning the most important region, the brokers who sell it, the courtiers (agents) who place the stock, and the customers who fight to buy it, all on their heads. Latour is a very wealthy property owned by a very wealthy man, the self-made billionaire and industrialist François Pinault, who also owns Yves St. Laurent, Gucci and Christie's Auction House. If anyone can afford to sit on some stock and then release it onto to the market when they decide (at much more expensive prices, of course, than they would have received in the 'en primeur' model) then it is the jewel in the Left Bank of Bordeaux's crown.

Château Latour is the most famous and revered of Bordeaux's Premier Crus. The 90ha estate sits just to the north of Château Pichon-Lalande, overlooking the mighty Gironde Estuary on the southern border of the Pauillac and northern border of the St.Julien communes. The famous tower on the label is not in fact the Château – which hides in the trees behind it – and it is one of the most famous landmarks in the entire wine world.

The wines are remarkably long-lived, often dark, brooding and impenetrable in their youth and are the epitome of the Cabernet Sauvignon grape variety. Some 10,000 cases of Latour's Grand Vin are made each year and this wine comes from a collection of plots in the heart of the property known as L'Enclos. Latour created a second wine in 1966, the immensely collectable and expensive Les Forts de Latour. Even the third wine, called Le Pauillac de Château Latour is a beautiful and impressive creation. In addition, Latour always pulls it off with so-called 'lesser' vintages, or those with more challenging weather conditions. We wine critics reward this integrity and flair. The skill of the winemaker, the endless hours in the vineyards nurturing the vines, the divine setting with its perfect soil and aspect and the ruthlessness of the owner or manager to de-classify sub-standard fruit makes Latour a paragon of perfection.

Dating back to 1331 the name Latour is thought to come from the Tor à Saint-Lambert garrison which was situated here. The original tower, which gave its name to the surrounding estate, was destroyed at the end of the Hundred Years War, but in the 1620s a circular tower, La Tour de Saint-Lambert, was built on the estate and rather than housing its architect or its owner it was actually designed as a pigeon roost. Wine was made on the estate during this time, too, and for nearly 300 years 'Latour' was passed down through the generations, via a number of interconnected families. Interestingly three centuries ago, in 1716, it was part of a portfolio which included Lafite and Montrose, and Calon-Ségur was added a few years later! Can you imagine this happening today? One of the world's most famous wine collectors Thomas Jefferson was, in the latter part of the 18th century, minister to France, and he noted that 'La Tour de Ségur' was 'a vineyard

of first quality'. Latour's reputation was already very strong by the beginning of the 18th century and it was exported to England alongside other soon to be First Growths Lafite and Margaux. This fêted status was bestowed on four Châteaux for the International Exhibition, held in Paris in 1855. From this moment onwards Latour, Lafite, Haut-Brion and Margaux secured their positions in history forever. Each one of these wines has their own character, and they all appear in this book. Latour is, however, the mightiest of the bunch and it never fails to leave an indelible mark on our taste memories. In 1963 the estate finally left the Ségur family, after them losing it

01 *Château Latour 1899: one of the greatest vintages*
02 *The Tower at Château Latour*

| 02

following the French Revolution and then manoeuvring cleverly to regain their interest afterwards. They sold Château Latour to the British Pearson Group, owners of the Financial Times and Harvey's of Bristol among other companies. It was during this period that a massive investment was made in research at Latour and the vineyards were expanded and also replanted where necessary. The chai (cellar) was extended and it has been further extended in 2002. Latour became the first of the Premier Crus to bring their winemaking and production up to true 20th century standards. In 1989 Latour was purchased by Allied Lyons, but four years later François Pinault stepped in and re-established French ownership.

I have never scored a bottle of Latour any lower than 18.5/20 (i.e. gold medal standard) in my notes – and I have tasted well over 40 vintages. Every single year, at the 'en primeur' tastings, Latour ranks in the top three or four estates in the whole of Bordeaux. It is, more often than not, my number one. This makes Château Latour, for me, the finest incarnation of Cabernet Sauvignon in the world. The elemental force of Latour is felt the moment that you step on the property and it is a life-changing feeling.

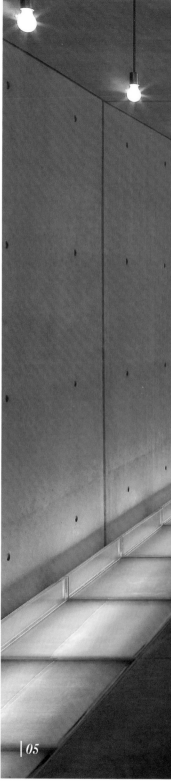

03   The door to the winery
04   Stainless steel vats
05   1st year cellar

*1er Cru
Margaux
Bordeaux*

Château Margaux

• Probably the most photographed building in the region, Château Margaux is a stunning 'castle' and it makes epic wines. A beacon of excellence and the only First Growth in the commune of Margaux, every wine that I taste from this property resonates around the senses, impressing with its heavenly texture and deliciousness. With more immediately seductive fruit but just as much longevity as all of the other stellar properties in the Left Bank, Margaux is in a different league. Owned by Corinne Mentzelopoulos the professionalism and dedication of the team at Margaux is second to none. They capture the essence of the vintage in the Grand Vin, as well as in the second wine Pavillon Rouge du Château Margaux, and the dry white wine Pavillon Blanc du Château Margaux, unusually made from 100% Sauvignon Blanc.

Château Haut-Brion

• The oldest of the five First Growths in Bordeaux and the only one situated in the outskirts of the town itself; Haut-Brion is the epitome of elegance and distinction and the wines have a character all of their own. Reserved and stylish, Haut-Brion is not as showy or opulent as many, preferring to open slowly in the glass and enrapture the taster with its complexity and phenomenal length. Haut-Brion makes a superb second wine called Le Clarence de Haut-Brion, after Clarence Dillon, the American banker, who bought the estate in 1935. Haut-Brion also produces a spectacular and very rare white wine which never fails to gain my top score for a dry white in the region every year. Haut-Brion also owns Château La Mission Haut-Brion, which makes magnificent red and white wines too.

Château Climens

"Climens is the finest estate in this region by some considerable margin and this is because the wines not only have fine Barsac purity, but they also have extraordinary length, refinement and persistence."

1er Cru
Barsac-Sauternes
Bordeaux
Established 16th century

|01

01   *Climens through the ages*
02   *Immaculately tended Semillon vineyard*

• This 30ha property, situated at the highest point of the Barsac commune (20m above sea level), some 40 kilometres from Bordeaux up the Garonne River, is one of the finest sweet wine producing estates in the world. It is here, in a unique microclimate, that the microscopic fungus Botrytis cinerea develops in the vineyards, clinging to the skins of the Semillon grapes, giving rise to the venerable-sounding and fortune-making 'Noble Rot'. Late in the season this rot attacks the bunches on the vines and the mouldy grapes are sucked dry of their water, leaving fuzzy looking bunches behind, with the most heavenly sugar imaginable locked safely inside each grape.

It is worth noting that Noble Rot is not the same as grey rot, which ruins crops and brings with it a mouldy flavour in the resulting wine. In Noble Rot's case the flavour of the wine is actually enhanced by this relatively unsightly invader and so it is encouraged. Why does this particular part of the world attract this peculiar rot so successfully? The answer lies in a tributary of the Garonne River called the Ciron, which bisects 'greater' Sauternes, separating Barsac in the north western corner of the region from the other sectors - Bommes, Fargues, Preignac and Sauternes itself. Just north of Preignac, this river slices through the countryside and, by dint of its cool waters, it brings the magical mistiness and early morning moisture which, coupled with autumnal sunshine, Botrytis ado res. It is, in effect, the most expensive source of divine atomiser in the world.

When the Noble Rot-affected grapes are crushed, sweet vinous elixirs emanate and after fermentation in oak barrels it makes the finest of all sweet wines. Barsac appellation wines have a distinct flavour which sets them apart from their near neighbours. Barsacs have freshness and lift on the nose and a palate that renders them more ethereal and sprightly than some of the more intensely tropical Sauternes. It is for this reason that many wine lovers search out Barsac wines in order to enjoy them not only with puddings, but also with terrines, foie gras and a wide variety of cheeses.

Climens is the finest estate in this region by some considerable margin and this is because the wines not only have fine Barsac purity, but they also have extraordinary length, refinement and persistence. I have been lucky enough to taste 1908 Château Climens and it was still crammed full of 'joie de vivre' and energy. Other well-known Barsac estates include Coutet, the only other Premier Cru, and also Doisy-Daëne, Doisy-Védrines, Broustet, Suau,

Nairac and Caillou, all Deuxièmes Crus. They are a worthy supporting corps to the captivating prima ballerina assoluta that is Climens. What is surprising about the wines from this part of the world is that in comparison to other great Bordeaux reds, they are sensational value. I always seem able to satiate my unquenchable thirst for Climens in spite of only 3000 or so cases being made each year.

Châteaux Climens is owned by Bérénice Lurton, from the famous Lurton wine dynasty. She took over management of Climens at 22 years of age, in 1992, when her Father Lucien announced one day that he was to retire and that his 10 children would have to look after his extraordinary collection of Châteaux. Bérénice has done an incredible job from a very young age and she likes to do things her way; ploughing a singular furrow which has elevated her to the ranks of president of the Association des Crus Classés de Sauternes

et Barsac. Planted exclusively to Semillon, a rare single varietal estate in the region because Sauvignon Blanc and Muscadelle are also planted, the 35-year-old vines dwell in the fascinating-sounding ferrous clay sand on fissured starfish limestone subsoil. Climens is one of the few estates

| 03

in the region to change to biodynamic viticulture. Bérénice took this leap of faith in 2010 and changed farming régimes en masse. Who knows what the future will hold, but I am certain that this will only further refine the offerings from this stellar estate.

Because of the nature of Botrytis, the yields are absolutely tiny in this form of wine production especially at Climens where the picking is obsessively meticulous - only 7 or 8 hectolitres/hectare (around a fifth of that of a red wine). The wine is fermented in oak barrels and the blending of the final wine is as ruthless as possible. In fact in 1984, 1987, 1992 and 1993 no Climens was released at all. In these years, another release called Cyprès de

Climens is produced which is a shimmering gem designed for earlier drinking, still engendering the majesty of the estate. Blossoming at around the 15-year mark Climens is a divine pleasure. This is one wine which is not big, bold, mouth-filling and luxuriant; it is however, elegant, graceful, ultra-refined, poised and subtle. I hope that you will feel compelled to taste Climens once you have read this chapter because, as I say to my friends when I pour this wine, you will be a better person for it and some of the molecules of flavour will never ever leave you.

04

05

03 *Château Climens world-class wine*

04 *Wine maturing in the barrel cellar at Château Climens*

05 *The facade of the chateau*

Château d'Yquem

- The greatest of all Sauternes and the most respected and collected of all sweet wines in the world, Château d'Yquem is a work of art. In spite of its profound sweetness, it starts off life incredibly quietly with a heavenly nose, but a firm, restrained palate. In time this blossoms, taking between 15 and 30 years to come about, and when it does you will find the experience completely life-changing. With 100 ha of vines you might expect a decent sized production, but with microscopic 9hl/ha yields it takes one vine to make just one glass of wine. Once tasted never forgotten; d'Yquem truly is liquid gold.

**1er Cru
Sauternes
Bordeaux**

Château Rieussec

• Owned by the Rothschilds and sitting in the same portfolio as Château Lafite, Rieussec is the polar opposite in flavour and deportment to the two other Sauternes in this book. With a rich, burnt orange colour and a heady aroma of marmalade and lusty wild honey, this is a wine which starts life with a firework of flamboyance and then never lets up on the pace. The ostentatious nose, drama-drenched palate and woozy finish are gripping and I find this beautiful combination of traits irresistible. In spite of its precocity, Rieussec ages extremely well and as the years tick by the enthusiastic primary fruit flavours fall away and a classy old dame remains.

Château Pétrus

- Château Pétrus is, without doubt, the most famous wine made from the Merlot variety in the world and it is also one of the most expensive and impossible to find in the fine wine market. The key to this wine's success is found in the vineyards. The soil at Pétrus, on the top of the Pomerol plateau in the eastern corner of the commune, is predominantly clay and the old Merlot vines love these conditions. Judicious viticulture focuses the energies of these vines into making a harvest worth its weight in gold. Pétrus is matured in 100% new oak barrels for two years and it is this full throttle winemaking which complements the velvety smooth Merlot fruit, giving it lustre and phenomenal generosity on the palate. The results are hypnotic and unforgettable. Sadly, only 2500 cases are made each year.

Vieux Château Certan

• The most suave and gentlemanly of the Pomerol superstars, VCC is one of the grandest of all wines in Bordeaux and it is owned and made by the supremely gifted Alexandre Thienpont. The 14ha estate is planted to Merlot, Cabernet Franc and a small amount of Cabernet Sauvignon and it is the interplay between Merlot and Cabernet Franc, principally, which creates the exquisite drama in the wines. With its erudite, aromatically complex, lithe wines VCC is a welcome break from the glossy, heady Pomerol/Merlot template. I remember drinking 1983 VCC in the early days of my career and it was wholly compelling and inspirational. On a recent trip to Bordeaux, Alexandre told me that he likes to make his wines 'on the cashmere side'. Having tasted many vintages I know exactly what he means.

1er Grand Cru Classé (A)
Saint-Emilion
Bordeaux

Château Cheval Blanc

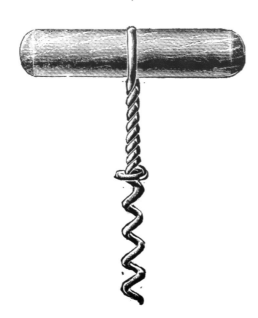

• With its new space age winery, counterpointing the elegant Château, Cheval Blanc manages to work the ancient and futuristic balance perfectly, as you might expect from a company that is owned by luxury goods empire LVMH. This is a property where the Cabernet Franc variety, with its glorious aromatics, plays a vital part in the blend alongside Right Bank stalwart and liquid velvet protagonist, Merlot. With a relatively large production of some 6000 cases of the Grand Vin and 2500 cases of the Second wine Le Petit Cheval, this is a property which makes a glorious impact globally. I am lucky enough not to have just tasted the legendary 1947 Cheval Blanc but to have drunk it, too. I can assure you that some of the recent vintages of this great Château show all of the splendour of old.

Château Ausone

• Ranked Premier Grand Cru Classé (A) in the Classification of Saint-Emilion, this incredible property is perched on the limestone cliffs beneath the town overlooking the valley below. The 7ha vineyards, on the slopes under the Château (and also above the winery which is cut into the rock), are planted with Cabernet Franc and Merlot and the production is a tiny 2000 cases. Ausone, which is named after Ausonius, the 4th century poet and writer on viticulture who was born in Bordeaux, is one of the most structured and arresting of all red Bordeaux. The colour is opaque, the weight and density of flavour both exceptional; revealing layers of complex fruit and minerality. Owner Alain Vauthier is a fastidious man and his painstaking renovations of the property show that he is a stickler for detail. This is also demonstrated by the commanding presence of his legendary wine.

Le Pin

"When tasting Le Pin I usually end up writing several pages of notes about one single sip, such is the complexity and all-enveloping experience"

Pomerol
Bordeaux
Established 1979

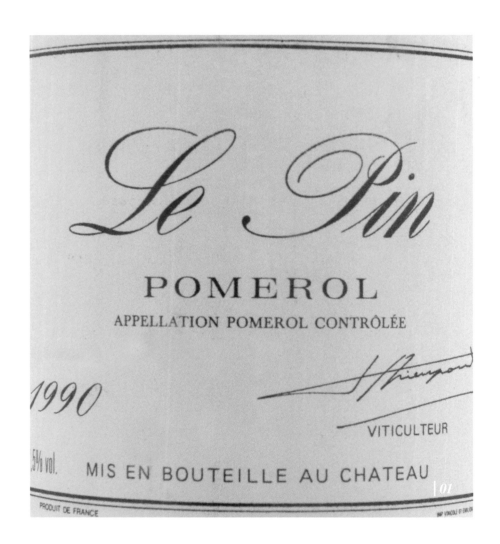

• I have long been a critic of the so-called garagiste movement which infected some Right Bank producers, in Bordeaux, in the late '80s and '90s. This fad of making small batch wine in your 'garage', involved using super ripe fruit, extended time in oak and other spurious tricks used to concentrate the flavours of the wines. The results were on the whole unpleasant. Soupy, oaky, high alcohol fruit bombs are not, to my mind, what the heavenly wines of Pomerol and Saint-Emilion should taste like. Winemakers, fuelled by the desire for massive scores and the accompanying fame and riches, temporarily forgot that the consumer actually had to drink the wines one day.

Le Pin has been cited as one of the front-runners of this trend, but this is categorically wrong. Yes, the wine is made in very small quantities and you could say that it is made in a garage of sorts (more of which later). It is also very expensive and oak certainly forms an important part of its makeup. Le Pin, named after a pine tree on the property, started off its life in 1979 and so the timing seems right, too, but several important factors need to be considered which should mean that Le Pin is never mentioned in the same sentence as the word garagiste again – damn, I just broke my own rule. This wine comes from a distinct, geologically atypical plot of land – hence it can only be made in small quantities. The soil is gravel and sand over clay and after acquiring a further hectare adjoining the winery, it is

now at its natural limit because there is no other patch of soil like it. The winery was designed to fit the size of land from which it takes its grapes – garage-sized granted, but only if you own a fleet of Bugatti Veyrons. Le Pin is also sublimely balanced, hedonistically appointed and exquisitely well-proportioned.

Jacques Thienpont is a member of the fabulous Thienpont wine dynasty which includes Alexandre, owner of nearby Vieux-Château Certan (q.v.) and Nicolas who runs Larcis Ducasse and Pavie Macquin, both in Saint-Emilion. Jacques bought just over one hectare of vines in the hamlet of Catusseau, in Pomerol, in 1979 from Madame Laubie, who in turn had owned it since 1924. A further hectare was acquired in the '80s. There was an old farmhouse on the property where Jacques made his 100% Merlot wine in the basement. This dowdy old building was replaced in 2011 by a striking, new, modern winery, designed by Belgian architect Paul Robbrecht and complete

with a tasting room and a tower. Inside, small stainless steel micro-cuves are used for fermentation, and gravity only moves the wine around. This doll's house-sized chai makes around 600 cases of wine per year. Le Pin's gravelly soil naturally promotes very low yields (30-35 hl/ha) and the first vintage appeared in 1979. One of the most sought-after and expensive wines in Bordeaux, Le Pin is a profound and intense joy.

Every time I taste with Jacques he is extremely generous, humble and welcoming; always opening two vintages to compare side by side. When tasting Le Pin I usually end up writing several pages of notes about one single sip, such is the complexity and all-enveloping experience you feel while you have Le Pin in your glass. Sadly, stellar prices (often several thousands of pounds per bottle) and extreme rarity mean that many of us will never get the chance to taste Le Pin, but don't despair because Jacques has come up with a new label called L'If, meaning the

yew tree. It is situated in Saint-Emilion, in two plots, near Château Troplong-Mondot. With 20% Cabernet Franc in the mix and being sold at a much lower price the Le Pin it is now possible to drink one of Jacques' wines at an attainable price. I suggest you put your feelers out now.

01 Le Pin 1990
02 Le Pin's winery

Georges Vernay

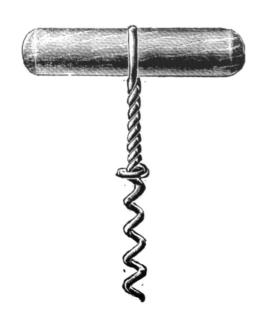

• This Condrieu specialist estate covers 7.5ha making it one of the three most important in the region. Run by George's daughter Christine and her husband Paul Ansellem they also make a small amount of beautiful Côte-Rôtie and Saint-Joseph, too. Their three distinct Condrieu cuvées are some of the most evocative expressions of the Viognier grape in the world. Coteau de Vernon comes from 60-year-old vines and is a model Viognier with an exquisite scent and sleek chassis. Les Chaillées de l'Enfer is a warmer site and the wines are more intense and heady with fig and nougat tones. Les Terrasses de l'Empire is the most forward and slim-line of the cuvées with a curvy but pliable body and precocious charm. You can also experience a Viognier, made by Christine, from the Collines Rhodaniennes, above the Condrieu appellation, called Le Pied de Samson – at half of the price of l'Empire and a third of Vernon it is a wine worth tracking down.

Crozes-Hermitage
Northern Rhône

Alain Graillot

• I remember drinking Alain Graillot's first vintage of Crozes-Hermitage, the 1985, in Willi's Wine Bar, in Paris, in 1988. It was the first time that I identified what I thought was the individual and unmissable purity of the Syrah grape from Crozes. The wines still have those incredible white pepper, iodine, tapenade and blackcurrant notes on the nose and palate today. These are very special wines indeed and if you crave top-flight Northern Rhône Syrah but don't want to wait an eternity for Hermitage, Cornas or Côte-Rôtie to mature then head to this Domaine immediately. Drinking perfectly from three years old these are insanely delicious wines. Keep your eyes peeled for Graillot's 'super-cuvée' La Guiraude which is a barrel selection made in top vintages – it is sublime.

E. Guigal

"The stroke of genius which propelled Guigal to the highest echelon of world winemaking was his decision to vinify some of his Côte-Rôtie wines as single vineyard offerings."

Côte-Rôtie
Northern Rhône
Established 1946

| 01

• Many people's first introduction to the famous Guigal name is via the terrifically reliable Guigal Côtes-du-Rhône. This 'one-wine messaging service' has communicated the family name faster and wider, and had more impact than any television or billboard advertisement, on the world's most faithful wine-loving public. Yet as delicious as this wine is, it is only the tip of the Guigal iceberg and further investigation yields some extraordinary flavours, aromas and many unforgettable memories.

Etienne Guigal started his career at Vidal-Fleury in 1924, at the age of 14, and he founded his own company in 1946, in Ampuis, a small, ancient village in the Côte-Rôtie appellation of the Northern Rhône. A diligent and fastidious worker, Etienne was suddenly struck with blindness and in 1961 his young son Marcel took control of the family business. Today the third generation of the family, Philippe, is the winemaker at Guigal and having spent time with him and his father, we can be assured that this dynasty, albeit a fairly short one by European standards, will be here for a very long time to come.

Guigal is known as the most famous producer of Côte-Rôtie, making over 40% of the wines from this mighty appellation. A great landmark for Guigal was the purchase of the famous Château d'Ampuis, in 1995, and it is now the Guigal HQ. This beautiful 12th century fort was renovated in the 16th century into a stunning Renaissance castle, situated on the banks of the Rhône. Having fallen into disrepair, the Guigals have completely renovated this vinous landmark and I have fond memories of filming a TV series there in 1998. On the eve of a massive dinner to celebrate the award of Marcel's 'Légion d'Honneur', he kindly walked me through the Château, pointing out the meticulous work they were doing in restoring every detail to its original splendour. It seems very fitting to me that this king of Côte-Rôtie should operate his fiefdom from such a famous monument.

Guigal has strategically augmented his vineyard holdings over the last few decades. Vidal-Fleury was the first acquisition in 1986 followed by Jean-Louis Grippat in 2001, Vallouit and also Domaine de Bonserine, as well as taking on countless other small parcels from local farmers. Making a large range of wines from the Southern and Northern Rhône, under both Domaine and Négociant labels, Guigal vinifies and ages all of his cuvées in a 3ha winery and cellars in Ampuis. The stroke of genius which propelled Guigal to the highest echelon of world winemaking was his decision to vinify some of his Côte-Rôtie wines as single vineyard offerings. This

'Burgundian' mentality was revolutionary and the world's collectors collectively sat up and paid attention. Guigal makes three single vineyard Côte-Rôties - La Landonne, La Mouline and La Turque, affectionately known as the 'LaLas'. They are some of the most expensive and rare wines made from Syrah (and Viognier) on the planet.

In short, Marcel Guigal single-handedly elevated the status of Côtie-Rôtie to that of the other Northern Rhône superstar appellation, Hermitage. Concentrating on low yields, organic viticulture and, curiously, maturing the wines for a very long time in new oak barrels (up to three and a half years) these wines are nothing short of hypnotic. La Landonne was first produced in 1978 and there are around 10,000 bottles made each year. It is the only 100% Syrah wine and it comes from within the Côte Brune 'lieu-dit'. Usually the most backward of the three, you shouldn't think about drinking a bottle until after its

15th birthday. La Mouline comes from a single parcel inside the 'lieu-dit' of Côte Blonde. The first vintage was 1966 and some 5000 bottles are made each year. This is often the most aromatic of the three on account of the large amount (10-11%) of the perfumed white grape Viognier used in the blend. La Turque also uses Viognier in the mix, but a lower percentage this time, and it comes from a plot in the Côte Brune. Its first vintage was 1985 and around 5000 bottles are produced. Style-wise it sits somewhere between La Mouline and La Landonne depending on the vintage. The

| 02

| 03

Château d'Ampuis cuvée was launched with the 1985 vintage and it sits below these three superstars. It is made from a blend of Côte Brune and Côte Blonde fruit and there is always a Viognier element involved, typically around 7%. The most widely available cuvée is Côte-Rôtie Brune et Blonde de Guigal, a 'négociant' wine, which manages to harness the uniqueness of the setting but also drinks a lot earlier than its loftier stable-mates. Guigal also has a major stake in the dreamy Viognier wines of the neighbouring appellation, Condrieu. Nearly one half of the 25,000 cases of this wine made each year are under his label, with Condrieu La Doriane being his flagship wine.

Further afield Guigal has serious plots of land in Saint-Joseph and Hermitage, with

Ermitage Ex-Voto red and white rivalling the very finest Domaines. We must all raise our glasses to Guigal and their wines – it is not often than one family transforms an entire wine region with their passion and commitment. They are true wine heroes.

| 04

| 05

Jean-Louis Chave

- Chave is a devastatingly serious producer of Hermitage. With 25 to 30 years in the engine for these exceptional wines there is no hurry to find a corkscrew and you mustn't let impatience get the better of you because the difference between a young Chave Hermitage and a mature one is stark. Coming from several different plots on the famed hillside this is one of the most elemental and inspirational wines made from the Syrah variety. Without the use of new oak found in many other estates' wines, the fruit moves slowly and with monumental determination. The prize is one of the most blissful flavours that your olfactory system could ever hope to process. That is, until you taste the Chave's white Hermitage. This is a wine that I put on the same plane as Haut-Brion Blanc and only a handful of Grand Cru white Burgundies – it really is that good. So why not get one of each? With a Saint-Joseph in the portfolio and a thoroughly worthy 'négociant' arm this is a busy and brilliantly reliable producer.

Auguste Clape

• Auguste, Pierre & Olivier Clape own five hectares of Syrah vines in Cornas, on the west bank of the mighty Rhône river, just above Saint Péray. I am not overstating the fact when I say that the wines from this little estate are some of the most captivating in the world. I remember an evening in Brisbane where I was hosting a Syrah masterclass dinner for some luminaries of the Aussie wine scene including James Halliday and the late, great Len Evans when I poured the 1990 vintage. It was the star of the evening, up against 1988 Chave Hermitage, Guigal's 1996 La Turque, 1994 La Mouline, La Landonne 1997 and

Penfolds Grange among others. It was also the least expensive wine opened on the night. Cue fanfare!

M. Chapoutier

"It's remarkable that Michel Chapoutier has created a multi-tiered empire with such amazing quality and integrity across the board. It is rare to see such commitment to all sectors of the wine-adoring public and he is to be applauded for his unwavering ambition."

Tain-l'Hermitage
Northern Rhône
Established 1808

| 01

• The Chapoutier family has been making wine in the Rhône Valley since 1808. Max Chapoutier retired in 1977 leaving his sons Michel and Marc to run the business and in the '80s their wines started to attract a lot of attention, appealing to a curious, fast-moving international market. They did what a lot of top French producers didn't - they relentlessly toured the world opening incredible bottles for their fans. This worked a treat and when the heady combination of haute cuisine and Chapoutier wines hit town everyone wanted an invitation.

The upward trajectory continued apace when Michel Chapoutier took over the reins of the company in 1990 and from this moment, the wines not only gathered more favourable reviews but also, for me, they started to truly sing about their precise origins – the Holy Grail of wine. I am certain that this is because Michel Chapoutier moved from being a fan of organic viticulture to a fervent advocate for farming biodynamically. This spiritual and cosmic vinous awareness allows each parcel of land to perform at its finely tuned best, and the resulting Chapoutier wines found definition and clarity as well as more obvious, impressive fruit flavours. The iconic Chapoutier Braille wine labels have been around since 1996. Maurice Monier de la Sizeranne, owner of the plot of the Hermitage La Sizeranne, which Chapoutier makes, invented the first version of abbreviated Braille. Chapoutier's labels pay tribute to him and also, uniquely, allow

sight-impaired wine lovers to locate their favourite cuvées!

Chapoutier has enviably extensive vineyard holdings in the prime Rhône appellations as well as making a handful of stunning, inexpensive wines in the Greater Rhône areas of Luberon, Tricastin and Ardèche. Michel even ventures outside of the Rhône to the Roussillon (Domaine Bila-Haut), Alsace, Australia and Portugal. He operates both as a 'négociant' and a Domaine and occasionally enters into partnerships with like-minded wine obsessives.

The Chapoutier HQ is in Tain-l'Hermitage and from here he conducts a mighty orchestra of labels. At the very top of the pile are his so-called 'Sélections Parcellaires'. These are the wines that attract the most attention and it is easy to taste why. All of these are site-specific creations and pure varietals – so there is no Viognier in the Côte-Rôtie, Roussanne in the white Ermitage or Syrah in the

Châteauneuf! This raft of amazingly concentrated and profound wines includes the Northern Rhône superstars Côte-Rôtie La Mordorée, Condrieu Coteaux de Chery, Crozes-Ermitage Les Varonniers, Saint-Joseph Les Granits (red and white) and an Ermitage portfolio that defies belief. Chapoutier owns around a quarter of the entire appellation. He favours the Ermitage spelling, losing the 'h' because this, to him, signifies that the wine is made from a single plot of vines as opposed to being blended from a series of 'lieu dits'. So within Hermitage, this is his list of Ermitages - De l'Orée, L'Ermite (red and white), Le Méal (red and white), Le Pavillon, Les Greffieux and even a Vin de Paille (straw wine). All of the reds are 100% Syrah; the whites are 100% Marsanne. They bulldozer the palate with their impact and then relentlessly romance your taste buds with their persistence and charm.

These are some of the most shocking and memorable wines in the world and it is this mighty backbone which supports the rest

of the business. In the Southern Rhône, he makes two Châteauneuf-du-Pape, Barbe Rac and Croix de bois, both 100% Grenache. This delineation and non-blending attitude allows us to focus clearly on the fruit expression and the exact GPS coordinates of the vineyards which, by definition, are totally and utterly unique. It is a thrilling experience.

01   *Braille labels*
02   *Hermitage vineyards*

Below these great wines is a series entitled 'Prestige' and these are made from his own fruit supplemented by bought parcels. These are the wines that are most visible on the market and they are restaurant favourites, too, being relatively forward and faithful to the time-honoured flavours associated with their names. All capture the heart and soul of the region and a few are superb value - Hermitage La Sizeranne (red), Hermitage Chante-Alouette (white), Condrieu Invitare, Côte-Rôtie Les Bécasses, Cornas Les Arènes, Crozes-Hermitage Les Meysonniers (red and white) and Châteauneuf-du-Pape La Bernadine (red and white). With my journalist hat on I often find myself writing up some of Michel's 'Tradition' range which is one step lower. This includes a Crozes-Hermitage Petite Ruche, St Joseph Deschants and a very smart Côtes-du-Rhône Belleruche. With my restaurant wine-buying hat on, some of his aforementioned Ardèche creations have worked beautifully as upmarket house wines.

It's remarkable that Michel Chapoutier has created a multi-tiered empire with such amazing quality and integrity across the board. It is rare to see such commitment to all sectors of the wine-adoring public and he is to be applauded for his unwavering ambition.

| 04

| 05

Vieux Télégraphe

"It is thrilling to bring your attention to a wine which delivers its message concisely and with magnificent clarity, just like its 1792 namesake."

Châteauneuf-du-Pape
Southern Rhône
Established 1898

01 *Vieux Télégraphe Châteauneuf-du-Pape*
02 *La Crau vineyard*

• Vieux Télégraphe is one of the most famous and revered estates in the Southern Rhône. It takes its name from an old telegraph station which stood on the property. In 1792 Claude Chappe designed a series of optical relay towers which used semaphore and binoculars to transmit news across the country. This was the first practical telecommunications system of the industrial age. Sadly, the tower has been demolished, but the special patch of land on which it stood, called the Plateau de la Crau, has been home to some very special vines since 1898 when Hippolyte Brunier established Domaine du Vieux Télégraphe.

A large property, with 65ha of red vines and 5ha of whites all planted on La Crau, this is one of the finest tracts of land in the region, benefitting from a particularly hot microclimate. It is here that the large, smooth 'galets roulés' stones are found in the vineyards. These 'hot stones' warm up in the sunshine during the day and then slowly release their heat into the soil at night. This geological peculiarity encourages richness and nobility in the wines. With a decent clutch of old vines, up to 65 years old, and a rolling average of vines of well over 35 years old, this estate is perfectly balanced and the wines reflect this in the glass.

Vieux Télégraphe's blend is the model for all classic Châteauneuf-du-Pape wines, with Grenache accounting for around two thirds of the mix, and the rest being made up of Syrah and Mourvèdre with a tiny dribble of Cinsault for good measure. Only four wines are made at this estate – two reds and two whites. Vieux Télégraphe red and white are made from the oldest vines and are the flagships, while red and white Le Télégramme is M. Brunier's second label.

It is important to stress that this estate has eschewed the fashions that come and go in the wine world. He is a firm believer in not over-oaking his wines and in making the very best estate wine possible, rather than slicing up his property into little chunks which would inevitably detract from the overall excellence of the main estate wine. While this has meant that he has avoided the spotlight that often falls on the extrovert or attention seeking producers, it has however made him a beacon of excellence for classicists, such as myself, who adore the heavenly purity, drive and authenticity of his wines.

He is also insistent that Grenache is the workhorse grape in his reds. This is crucial because, once again, other properties have deflected from the time-honoured recipe of the Grenache-dominant blend in search of high scores and short term gain. Grenache doesn't hold all of the weapons though and so Mourvèdre, Syrah, Counoise and Cinsault join in and for the whites, the talented team of Clairette, Roussanne, Bourboulenc, Picpoul and Grenache Blanc all play their part. The sensitive layering of flavour in the Brunier wines brings an innate complexity to the finished article while our taste buds try to unravel each and every nuance. The cellars are situated at Le Pigeoulet, two kilometres to the south of the vineyard where, in a cooler spot, they are hewn into the rock. This offers perfect conditions for making and aging wine as well as taking advantage of gravity to allow for minimal pumping and handling. The vinification at Vieux Télégraphe is disarmingly straightforward. After destemming and pressing, the juice is fermented in temperature-controlled stainless steel tanks. It is then matured in concrete tanks prior to blending for up to a year and then in large oak 'foudres' (60 hectolitre barrels) for a further year. The wines are then bottled, unfiltered, and released on to the market. This elaborate technique that steers clear of technology has brought the wines a truth which reflects Le Crau and the character of the vintage. Nothing is more important when it comes to creating accurate and worthwhile wines.

The white wine is Clairette and Grenache Blanc-dominant with Roussanne and also Bourboulenc playing a vital part in the makeup. Barriques are used for the white wine to soften the palate a touch. The result is a stunning cocktail of honeysuckle, stone fruit and nougat with a taut citrus finish.

| 02

Vignobles Brunier, headed up by Daniel Brunier, is a hard-working and diligent wine making entity and they have expanded to include another Châteauneuf-du-Pape estate, this time making more flamboyant reds, coming from a collection of different terroirs, at Domaine la Roquète. In addition to this they run another paean to old Grenache vines at Domaine Les Pallières, in Gigondas. These are divine wines, too. There is one more wine in the Brunier portfolio which offers early drinking and immense enjoyment – Le Pigeoulet. It is made from about one third Châteauneuf-du-Pape and two thirds comes from the Côtes du Ventoux area, in the municipality of Caromb. A chip off the old block, Le Pigeoulet is about as posh as house wine gets and it allows you to graduate in style when you move on to open a bottle of Vieux Télégraphe.

In an age when I think that we all secretly crave the simplicity of a pair of binoculars and two flags to send a message, it is thrilling to bring your attention to a wine which delivers its message concisely and with magnificent clarity, just like its 1792 namesake.

| 03

| 04

03   *Salle à Foudre*
04   *Entrance to cellar*
05   *Old bottles of Vieux Télégraphe*

Beaucastel

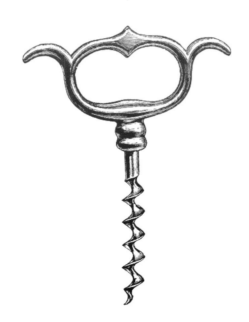

• Arguably the most famous estate in the region, the Perrin family has made a concerted push to further heighten the appeal of its flagship Châteauneuf-du-Pape wine of late, and the results are amazing. From Coudoulet, the 'second' wine which trumps most producers Grand Vins, to the earthy, meaty Châteauneuf-du-Pape itself, these are wines which use the full template of 13 varieties to great effect. The whites made at Beaucastel are also exceptional with the Roussanne Vieilles Vignes coming from a plot of vines planted in 1909. This is a truly great cuvée and one which should be drunk alongside stellar Chardonnays to compare and contrast their dramatic flavours. Finally there is the Hommage à Jacques Perrin, only made in top vintages. With a large dose of Mourvèdre and made in tiny quantities, this is an icon well worth tasting for its unique palate and sensational texture.

Tempier

• Owned by the Tempier family since 1834 this is my favourite producer of Provence's star red wine Bandol by some distance. The white and rosé are delectable wines but the real excitement is found in the unequalled portfolio of reds. Cuvée Classique is the starting point and this is a benchmark Mourvèdre-dominant red with a smattering of Grenache, Syrah and Carignan thrown in for good measure. An early-drinking, romantic and evocative wine, this is the base on which the other heroic wines stand. La Migoua is an amphitheatre-shaped 6ha vineyard which makes a wine with only 50% Mourvèdre and more Cinsault and Grenache in the mix. It's an earthy animal-scented creature made for rich pagan stews and game. La Tourtine is a Mourvèdre-dominant wine with a pronounced red fruit nose, more perfume and dextrous flashes of stylish leather and spice. This is my favourite cuvée for all-round pleasure. The final wine is Cabassaou, with very low yields and a monstrous 95% Mourvèdre. This inky, age-worthy wine is the standard bearer for the estate and it is a magnificent and daunting creature.

Germany

Karthäuserhof

"I would wager that this extraordinary hill will continue to yield some of the finest Riesling in the world for centuries to come."

Ruwer Valley
Mosel
Established 1811

| 01

01   *Karthäuserhof's iconic neck label*
02   *Wasserburg*

• I have only visited Christoph Tyrell once at his unique monopole estate, Eitelsbacher Karthäuserhofberg (meaning hill of the Carthusians) in the Ruwer Valley tributary of the Mosel River. During little over an hour I tasted his whole range of wines and gave out more stellar scores than at any other estate in my life. Thinking back to this day, I was profoundly affected by the tasting and it put delicate Mosel Riesling on a higher plane in my mind than I ever expected. Christoph was the perfect host and he didn't say an awful lot; leaving the wines to permeate my system and work their magic for themselves. I hit a 20/20 in my notes early in the tasting and ended up going above this perfect score because I had run out of headroom. The simple premise at this estate is that they hand-tend, hand-pick, hand-make and hand-bottle every single wine themselves. The team here knows all of the disciplines of their colleagues and they are a very well-drilled and faithful unit. The vineyard is owned exclusively by the family and it is made up of weathered Devonian slate at an angle of up to 45%. This slate retains heat during the day and clay deposits in the soil retain water, so this vineyard has the perfect makeup for performing at the highest level in even the most challenging vintages. The rose-red coloured slate is responsible for imbuing the most extraordinary minerality in the range of Rieslings and Pinot Blancs made here.

A Weissburgunder Trocken (dry Pinot Blanc) kicks off the range and is as pure as can be. All of the other wines are made from Riesling and there are masses of them across all styles. From Kabinett, to Kabinett Feinherb (with more ripeness, similar to an old Halbtrocken), to Spätlese, Auslese, Beerenauslese and Eiswein, this sliding scale of sweetness and rarity is utterly compelling. You will see that on some of the very sweet wines there is a Fuder number and this relates to the barrel from which the wine came. While the forward drinking dry Kabinett wines are eminently affordable, at everyday prices, the Eisweins can reach several hundred pounds a bottle, such is their rarity.

The main difference between all of these wines is their level of sweetness: they come from slightly different parts of the vineyard and were picked at different times. The dryer wines are harvested first and the very sweet ones are picked late into the winter. All are fermented in stainless steel and the forward styles are bottled right away, while the very sweet styles lounge in old oak barrels (fuder) until bottling. So, unlike traditional winemaking, this single vineyard experiences innumerable passages through the vineyard by the pickers; harvesting exactly the right bunches for each specific style of wine and then waiting a few more days and doing the same for another style. The image of a vineyard being used over and over again to make such a large range of wines is baffling and fascinating in equal measure. That all of the wines have exactly the same intense slate-y notes and pristine purity of fruit is not surprising (because of

| 02

their source) but it is the sheer beauty and length of flavour that sets this estate apart from the rest. The other remarkable point about this winery is that they use the smallest labels you have ever seen. In fact they are neck labels and when a bottle is served you might think that the real label has fallen off in the ice bucket. However, on closer inspection you can see that all of the information is neatly included on the neck label.

Karthäuserhof celebrated its 200th anniversary in 2011 and with a recent archaeological find proving that the Romans also made wine here I would wager that this extraordinary hill will

continue to yield some of the finest Riesling in the world for centuries to come.

Mosel

Joh. Jos. Prüm

• JJ Prüm is the only one of these estates who I have asked to visit and who has turned me down (not sure of the reason), but this hasn't stopped their inclusion in this book because the wines are just too good to leave out. The estate is 100 years old and is widely regarded as the finest in the country. Almost singularly famous for the wines from the Wehlener Sonnenuhr vineyard across all sweetness levels including the rare goldkapsel (literally gold capsule) wines, these are celestial, highly sophisticated Rieslings. The 13.5ha estate, with nearly 70% ungrafted vines, also includes holdings in Zeltinger Sonnenuhr, Graacher Himmelreich, Graacher Domprobst, Bernkasteler Lay and Bernkasteler Badstube and all of these wines last for aeons. You never know, I might actually have the chance to taste the full range one day!

Dr. Loosen

• Ernst Loosen runs one of the greatest estates in Germany. Based just outside Bernkastel, with a large collection of old vines over 12ha, he makes some of the most intriguing and mesmerising wines in the country. Watch out for the following wines (listed village first, vineyard second) Erdener Treppchen, Erdener Prälat, Urziger Würzgarten, Wehlener Sonnenuhr, Bernkasteler Lay and Graacher Himmelreich at a full range of different sweetness levels. With encouragingly low yields and mercurial winemaking, Erni manages to imbue more strength of character and bravado into his wines, making the sweeter cuvées less cloying and more mineral-soaked than those of his peers. The sweet spot of value, complexity and drinkability that I look for is the Auslese level, between five and 10 years of age. I would pitch in around this point and then head sweeter and older when you are feeling thoroughly acclimatised.

Austria

Franz Hirtzberger

• My favourite producer(s) of both Riesling and Grüner Veltliner in Austria are father and son team of Franz Senior and Junior Hirtzberger. Their 12ha estate is situated in the south-western end of the Wachau on excruciatingly steep terraces, looking down on the Danube. The wines made here sing of their precise site and their incomparable beauty and this is down to the incredible work done in the vineyard by their guardians, the Hirtzbergers. Riesling Smaragd Singerriedel is the pinnacle of production wine here, but the portfolio is star-studded. Rieslings Hochrain and Setzberg also perform with balletic grace and power, and Grüners Axpoint and Honivogl redefine the upper echelons of potential and complexity for this wistful variety.

Moric

• Roland Velich started his Moric project in 2001. He doesn't own any vines, preferring to enter into contracts with growers who own very old (alte reben) Blaufränkisch vines. His intention is to reflect their soil and site in his profound wines. Velich's shamanic mastery of the Blaufränkisch grape always leaves me flabbergasted. His wines have all of the elements of my favourite red grapes rolled into one - Pinot Noir fruit purity and majesty, Nebbiolo finesse and tannin structure, and Syrah spice and presence. His Neckenmarkt Alte Reben and Lutzmannsburg Alte Reben wines are works of pure genius with soaring fruit flavours underpinned with debauched, musky notes. If you have never tasted the Blaufränkisch variety before, you must start here.

Italy

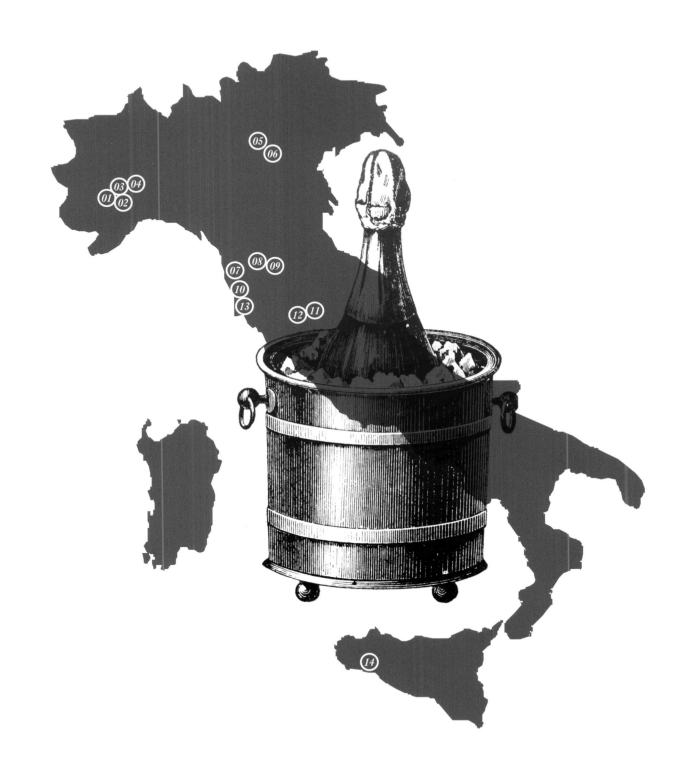

Elio Altare

• I am not using the word 'legend' lightly when I write this about Elio Altare. His Barolos are sublime and his mentoring of the young guns in Piedmont has changed the local landscape forever. He is considered to be one of the most forward-thinking and subtle of Barolo producers thanks to his deft use of French oak barriques. He likes to craft his Nebbiolo wines in the same shape and size as the great Pinot Noirs of Burgundy. This means that you can approach them earlier; that they are fine, long and sensual and that the tannins are grainy without being brutal. His Barolos Vigneto Arborina, Brunate and

Ceretto are the equivalent of ultra-fine Grand Crus and just as expensive, but don't forget that he also makes an incredibly well-priced Barbera, Dolcetto and a clutch of Lange Nebbiolos. Explore these wines and you will never look back.

Aldo Conterno

• Aldo Conterno recently passed away and I will never forget the lunch I enjoyed with him after tasting his extraordinary range of wines. In 1961, Conterno and his brother Giovanni inherited the Giacomo Conterno winery. Eight years later they split up, with Aldo creating his own estate - Poderi Aldo Conterno - in Bussia in Monforte d'Alba. A classicist at heart, Aldo didn't mind dabbling in some newfangled techniques. So by the 70s, endeavouring to tame the famed Nebbiolo tannins, he reduced fermentation lengths and changed from the submerged cap method in favour of gentler pumping over. These may sound old hat now, but at the time they were tantamount to heresy! One thing he wouldn't change was the use of large Slavonian oak barrels. He left barriques for his young rivals and continued to make his revered, age-worthy Barolos Granbussia Riserva, Romirasco, Cicala and Colonnello in his traditional style - and I am delighted that he stuck to his guns.

Barbaresco
Piedmont

Gaja

• Giovanni Gaja founded his wine estate over 150 years ago. Four generations later, one of the most switched on and charismatic movers in the wine business, Angelo Gaja, continues to amaze fans with his sensational Barolos and Barbarescos. His low-yielding, single vineyard wines kicked off the vogue long before others followed and he has set the pace for the progressive winemakers of Piedmont. His Barbarescos, Sorì San Lorenzo, Sorì Tildìn and Costa Russi are legendary. His Barolos Sperss, Conteisa, Dagromis are also heroic. But, it is his modern, rule-flouting cuvées which have attracted the most column inches and - in most cases - praise from those who taste them. Darmagi is a Cabernet Sauvignon-dominant Bordeaux blend, sold as Langhe Rosso. Sito Moresco is a pioneering Nebbiolo/Cabernet/Merlot blend while Gaia & Rey is a Piemontese Chardonnay and Alteni di Brassica is a Sauvignon Blanc! Wild, unhinged or just pure genius – you decide.

La Spinetta

● I have long been a fan of Giorgio Rivetti and his magnificent portfolio of incredible wines. Having just taken on the management of the famous Contratto Metodo Classico wines in addition to his Casanova Tuscan estate, he has a lot on his plate, but it is his Piedmont wines which have gained him his place in this book. From the shockingly pure Barbera Ca' di Pian and the majestic swagger of Barbera Gallina, to the vital, nervy Nebbiolo Langhe via noble Barolos Campè and Garetti and his stellar flight of Barbarescos Gallina, Starderi and Valeirano. These wines win massive scores in my notes and give me more pleasure than I can explain in mere words. Before signing off from this distinguished producer it is worth noting that Giorgio also makes my two favourite Moscatos, too – Biancospino and Bricco Quaglia. What a multi-talented and inspirational genius he is.

Allegrini

"This company makes some of the most vital and rewarding wines in the whole of Italy. It is rare to find a top restaurant without their wines on the list; they're widely admired by sommeliers, chefs and restaurateurs."

|01

01 *Allegrini's flagship wine,*
    Amarone
02 *Villa della Torre, a jewel of*
    Italian Renaissance architecture,
    now venue for Allegrini tastings
    and events

• The Allegrini family has been making wine in the Veneto since the 16th century. Based in Valpolicella, (which translates as 'valley of many cellars') the father of the company was Giovanni Allegrini. Giovanni was a pioneer whose faith in

his Valpolicella vineyards established the foundation of his family's world-famous wine business. After Giovanni's untimely death in 1983, the company was inherited by his three children, who ran it together for 20 years until his eldest son Walter passed away in 2003. Today, his brother Franco manages the vineyards and winemaking and his sister Marilisa masterminds Allegrini's marketing and communications. This company makes some of the most vital and rewarding wines in the whole of Italy. It is rare to find a top restaurant without their wines on the list; they're widely admired by sommeliers, chefs and restaurateurs. Allegrini is my favourite producer of two historic styles of wine – Valpolicella Classico and Amarone Della Valpolicella Classico.

All the Allegrini wines come from their 100ha Estate spanning the three towns of Sant'Ambrogio, San Pietro in Cariano and Fumane. Each of their vineyard sites brings a different element to the final wines. Palazzo della Torre, situated in the foothills of Fumane, is named after the beautiful Renaissance property, Villa della Torre, also owned by the family. Planted between 1962 and 1989 this 26ha vineyard sits at an average altitude of 240m and is responsible for Palazzo della Torre wine made from Corvina, Rondinella and a touch of Sangiovese. It is made using the ripasso method, which involves 'building' the intensity of the wine by fermenting it a second time with the introduction of juice

| 02

gathered from partially dried grapes. This technique results in a heavenly, mouth-coating style of Valpolicella. La Grola is the other historic Valpolicella vineyard in the portfolio. Located in the town of Sant'Ambrogio, this 30ha site is one of the finest in the land. Successive operations to increase the planting density here have resulted in a sky-rocketing of the quality of the grapes harvested and this special micro-climate is home to the world famous La Grola wine. Made from Corvina and Syrah, this is one of the most interesting Cru of the region. On the summit of the La Grola hill lies the 2.65ha vineyard that produces the flagship red of the same name, La Poja. Planted in 1979, Giovanni Allegrini identified this as the exact position for him to make his dream 100% Corvina masterpiece. Sitting on the top of the hill, the soil is very poor, stony and high in limestone; the whiteness of the surface acts as a mirror under the vines reflecting the rays of the sun back onto the bunches of grapes. This results in incredible ripeness and complexity - La Poja is the finest version of pure Corvina that I have ever tasted.

Allegrini's Amarone is the most majestic and harmoniously balanced in the region. Made from 100% partially dried grapes, which lose around 40% of their volume over the three or four-month process, this intense, rich, chocolate and prune-scented wine is utterly heavenly. So many Amarone styles are parched, with hot alcohol,

sinewy fruit and a medicinal aftertaste. Allegrini's version is the embodiment of luxury. A Recioto della Valpolicella Classico is also made and named after Giovanni Allegrini himself. This sweet red style is balanced to perfection by the stellar talents of his son Franco.

In addition to these famous sites, several other properties have joined the portfolio to bolster production of the wines. Villa Cavarena was once the home of Abbot Bartolomeo Lorenzi, an important Veronese poet and scholar. Allegrini bought the dilapidated 18th century villa and is completely restoring its vineyards. At an enviable altitude of 500m and with 20ha of

vineyards, this will be an amazing addition to the company when the vines are mature. Three further sites - Fieramonte, situated in Mazzurega, and Monte dei Galli and Villa Giona, both in the town of San Pietro in Cariano are also recent additions. This continued investment and forward-planning ensures that with climate variations and differing harvests, this company can raise the bar yet further.

While the source of the fruit is second to none, the winemaking here is remarkably sensitive, too. The introduction of French barriques to complement the large Slovenian botti has helped the wines enormously as well as the shorter time spent in oak allowing the complex flavours to express themselves fully. Radical efforts have gone into perfecting the appassimento technique of drying grapes to make Ripasso and Amarone. Franco's continued work on all of these elements is inspirational and there are many now following his lead. In 2007, Franco took the brave step to forgo the Classico status of his delicious entry level Valpolicella by bottling it under screw cap. This was a radical move as very few in Italy have taken the plunge with this excellent closure because it contravenes the wine laws. Typically, Franco's thoughts were only about the quality of his wine and in order to protect it from rogue corks and the resulting cork taint, he felt that he had no choice. The wine trade and the Allegrini fans have acted as one and responded by supporting this move and drinking more wine.

My final word goes to Marilisa. Allegrini is the only winery in Italy to post me a Christmas card each year. This thoughtful and touching act is proof that this winery cares enormously about its fans and its friends.

03 *Dried grapes resulting from the appassimento process, essential for producing Amarone and Recioto*

04 *The Devil: one of Villa's four giant gargoyle-style fireplaces*

05 *View of the hill 'La Grola', with 'La Poja' on its summit. In the background: Lake Garda*

Pieropan

"Over four generations this dedicated family has perfected the art of making stunning wines in a region which has very few standout heroes."

Soave
Veneto
Established 1890

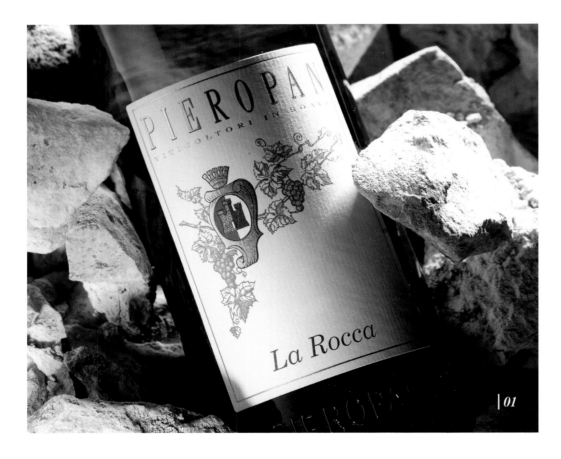

• Pieropan is the preeminent winemaker in Soave and it was founded by Leonildo Pieropan. Over four generations this dedicated family has perfected the art of making stunning wines in a region which has very few standout heroes. You will usually see mass-produced Soave populating supermarket shelves rather than fine wine merchants', but Pieropan's wines dwell in private collections, chic boutiques and on the finest dining tables in the world. Pieropan started producing white wine in the 1860s and this family firm was, in fact, the very first to bottle a wine with the word Soave on the label, in the early 1930s.

Today, Nino Pieropan, his wife Teresita and his sons Andrea and Dario run the estate. While they have some vineyard holdings in neighbouring Valpolicella, it is the pristine, crystalline whites from their home in Soave which captivate my palate. At the lower end of the scale, their Soave Classico, made from Garganega and Trebbiano is the benchmark for all others to aspire to. There are plenty of estates whose top wines are not as focused and serene as this cuvée. Above this wine are two di stinct Soave Classicos, both of which I follow extremely closely indeed. Firstly Calvarino, the first single vineyard Soave in existence, bottled over 40 years ago, in 1971.

The name is derived from the vineyard itself, 'Little Calvary'; reflecting the difficulty of getting from the bottom to the top and working between the vines. The basalt soils

01 *La Rocca wine and the typical clay soil on which its vineyards grow*
02 *Soave Classico vineyards*

here give the wine a distinct, taut, mineral theme. Beautiful and demure in its youth, this wine ages elegantly over six or seven years, but you mustn't feel guilty about drinking it young, because I do and it is tremendously rewarding. The Garganega and Trebbiano grapes in Calvarino are often picked in two distinct passages through the vines, ensuring that every grape is optimally ripe. Fermented and aged in glass-lined concrete tanks the structure of the wine is assembled via its contact with its lees, nothing more. The integrity and complexity of Calvarino comes direct from the vineyard itself and I buy it every year.

The other fabulous cuvée comes from the La Rocca vineyard. Situated on the Monte Rocchetta hill, just underneath Soave's medieval fortress, this vineyard is responsible for rich, structured, age-worthy Soave. Made exclusively from Garganega and first released in 1978, this is the 'Grand Cru' in the portfolio and you must try to exercise some restraint, only drinking it from six years of age onwards. This time 60% to 70% of the wine is aged in 500 litre oak casks and 30% to 40% is aged in 2000 litre botti for 12 months. The oak flavour is barely perceptible, but the amplitude that it brings to the wine is staggering. The next stunning Pieropan release is Le Colombare, a Recioto di Soave. Made from late-picked grapes, from the most exposed parts of the bunches, Recioto benefits from the grapes being partially dried on bamboo mats for five months and then aged for two years in large casks before release.

The Pieropans have made Recioto for over 100 years and it is their own favourite wine in the line up! Aging like clockwork, this is one of the most restrained sweet wine styles that you could drink with a game terrine or foie gras as much as a fruity pudding. However, if you are looking for a wine to complement your cheese course then the final expression from the La Rocca vineyard will have you gasping for a glass. Passito della Rocca is another dried grape style wine, but this time made from 50% Sauvignon Blanc, 30% Riesling with the balance being made up with Garganega and Trebbiano. The grapes are dried for approximately three months followed by fermentation and two years aging in French oak barriques. This makes for a decadent surprise; the old gold colour, and honey, dried fruit and nut notes are sensational. This style of sweet wine, with its gripping natural acidity and lusty fruit, makes for a very talented and food-friendly wine indeed.

02

These five unique wines from this small family company are unmissable. In addition to the operation in Soave, they have also started a new business in Valpolicella. With vines planted in 2000 they make a Valpolicella called Ruberpan and an Amarone della Valpolicella, too. With their undoubted pedigree in Soave and magical touch, I would urge you to keep a close eye on these two new Valpolicellas - there is every chance that this dedicated family will crack the codes of white, sweet white and also red wines, too!

03 Mr. Nino Pieropan and son Andrea checking Garganega grapes drying for Recioto di Soave Le Colombare

04 Valpolicella vineyard

05 New winery Villa Cipolla Pieropan where red wines are produced

| 04

| 05

Castello del Terriccio

• Castello del Terriccio can be found in the province of Pisa, 30 kilometres from the city itself, in the very northernmost part of the Tuscan Maremma. A little off the beaten track but well worth the journey, this estate makes two of my favourite wines in Italy, Lupicaia and Tassinaia under the guidance of the Master Winemaker Carlo Ferrini. Lupicaia is a Cabernet Sauvignon/ Merlot/Petit Verdot blend and it tastes of bitter chocolate, cinnamon, plums and black cherries. Tassinaia blends Cabernet, Sangiovese and Merlot for an epic and all-enveloping sensory explosion. Both of these Super Tuscans are from the very finest of top drawers and I heartily recommend them to you. With Chardonnay, Sauvignon Blanc and Syrah all grown on the property and even a very posh rosé you really must introduce yourself to Terriccio.

Chianti Classico
Tuscany

Isole e Olena

• The two villages Isole and Olena were joined to make one property by the De Marchi family in the '50s. Since 1976, Paolo De Marchi has run his 45ha estate making some of the best wines in Tuscany. His Chardonnay Collezione De Marchi is a joyous, silky, tropical wine with a long, sultry finish. He also makes an elegant Syrah and a sprightly Cabernet, but it is his Chianti Classico which displays sensational purity and élan. Above this wine is his Super Tuscan, Cepparello, which is bottled under both screw cap and cork, showing that Paolo is very much a man of the world. Cepparello is a tour de force that is incredibly enticing in its youth but that ages extremely well, too. One last wine made here is truly world-class – the Vin Santo which displays traditional dried grape notes and barrel nuances alongside a heady cocktail of exotic fruit and spice. Isole e Olena has a handful of brilliant wines which I urge you to taste.

Castello di Fonterutoli

"The reason for Fonterutoli's inclusion in this book is not because of the halo effect that they have cast over their other wines businesses, but the extraordinary quality of the wines made in Chianti Classico."

Chianti Classico
Tuscany
Established 1435

• Legend has it that in the early 13th century, the Lords of Florence and Siena decided to determine their common border in the Chianti region by organising a horse race. When the cock crowed, a knight would set out from each city riding towards each other and their meeting point would mark the border. The Florentines cunningly chose an emaciated black cockerel, which was on its last legs and desperate for a feed. Not surprisingly, this rooster crowed long before dawn and so the Florentine knight had a huge head start. He covered a great distance before meeting his rival on the outskirts of Siena, at Fonterutoli. Since then, the black rooster has been the emblem of the wines of Chianti. The Castle of Fonterutoli has been owned by the Mazzei family since 1435, but they have been involved in winemaking in the region since the 11th century. In fact, Ser Lapo Mazzei is considered to be the 'father' of the Chianti name. He wrote the first known document using this denomination and bearing his signature, dated 16th December 1398.

Another Mazzei, this time Filippo Mazzei (1730-1816) was asked by his wine-loving friend Thomas Jefferson to plant a vineyard at his estate in Monticello, Virginia. There are many more historic, eureka moments associated with this family, but it is today's Lapo, who oversees the property with the help of his sons Filippo and Francesco. They run the estate at Fonterutoli and also two

further wine properties, both making extremely impressive wines, in Maremma (Belguardo) and Sicily (Zisola).

The reason for Fonterutoli's inclusion in this book is not because of the halo effect that they have cast over their other wine businesses, but the extraordinary quality of the wines made in Chianti Classico. Even the entry level wine, Badiola, is thoroughly delicious. This crunchy cherry-style Sangiovese, blended with Merlot and Cabernet Sauvignon, is a welcome refuge in an ocean of largely indifferent inexpensive Chianti. Keep your eyes peeled for this wine on restaurant wine lists – it will no doubt get you out of a tight spot. One step above this wine is the Chianti Classico itself made from 90% Sangiovese with 10% being made up from Malvasia Nera, Colorino and Merlot. This is a benchmark Chianti and it is the wine that does the legwork for the brand internationally. With over 120 parcels of vines, this is a producer who can afford to choose the very best and while

Filippo and Francesco are undoubtedly charismatic chaps with film star looks and impeccably tailored suits, they would have struggled to gain the listings and following that they have, without this wine impressing everyone who tastes it.

Above this level there are still three more wines and these are the creations which have ensured this estate's position in this century of legendary wine producers. Ser Lapo Chianti Classico Riserva, named after the great man mentioned above, is the Riserva level Chianti and it sees a little more new oak and accordingly sports more intensity of fruit. More of a keeper than the straight Chianti Classico, this is a wine that will mellow beautifully with time. Next we come to the spectacular Castello de Fonterutoli Chianti Classico, which is a true masterpiece. Using even more new French oak (60%) and for a longer period of around 16 months, this wine loads complexity onto the palate via its use of 36 different clones of Sangiovese blended

01   *The legendary Chianti Classicos from Fonterutoli*

02   *One of the most important vineyards in the Chianti Classico region*

with 15% of Cabernet Sauvignon and Merlot. This diversity of material brings infinitesimal detail and nobility to the palate of this wine. It is one of the great wines of the region and I have been a massive fan of this cuvée for over 15 years.

Finally, there is a Super-Tuscan wine in the portfolio called Siepi, made from 50% Sangiovese and 50% Merlot. Having been privileged to conduct several vertical tastings of Siepi over the years, I can confidently put this wine in the very highest echelons of reds in Tuscany. With silky tannins, stunning length and also the élan that one associates with this particular estate, Siepi is a wine that will take Fonterutoli well into its 25th generation of Mazzeis in effortless style.

| 03

| 04

03   *Bottle archive*

04   *Temperature-controlled barrel cellar*

05   *Grape picking in vineyard*

Sassicaia

"This estate is responsible for changing the mind-set of the entire Italian wine business. This is a weighty statement but Sassicaia put Italy, its cultural vinous history and its wine laws under a global wine microscope."

Bolgheri
Tuscany
Established 1948

of Bolgheri to Tenuta San Guido. It sets the pulse racing as you arrive down this splendid drive and when tasting the wines made here you realise that you are somewhere very special indeed. Fast-forward 150 years from the planting of this avenue and you come to the moment when this estate dipped its toe in the wine business. When Clarice della Gherardesca married wine lover Mario Incisa della Rocchetta, the beginnings of Sassicaia, which means 'stony field', were born.

This estate is responsible for changing the mind-set of the entire Italian wine business. This is a weighty statement but Sassicaia put Italy, its cultural vinous history and its wine laws under a global wine microscope. I would venture that this terrific Tenuta made every estate re-evaluate what they were doing in the late 70s and early 80s and why. Collectively the country seemed to raise its game when Sassicaia became the talk of every town. This historic estate not only put the region of Bolgheri on the map, but it also created the first Bordeaux-style red wine in Italy. Tenuta San Guido is the home of the very first 'Super Tuscan' wine – as these brooding, expensive, age-worthy creations, made from non-indigenous grapes, became known.

Sassicaia was created by Mario Incisa della Rocchetta, a keen wine connoisseur of the Piemontese wines, where he grew up, and also of the great Bordeaux. His inspiration came from one of his illustrious

01 *Various vintages of Sassicaia, including the "Vino diverso", produced for a couple of years by Mario Incisa*

02 *Panoramic view of the "Aia Nova" vineyard, facing west*

• Now a protected and famous landmark, the entrance to this historic estate couldn't be more distinguished. A magnificent, three-mile avenue of cypress trees, planted in the early 1800s by Guidalberto della Gherardesca, takes you from the village

ancestors, great-grandfather Leopold, who catalogued, in great detail, two tomes of Italian and foreign vines. In 1948, Mario used his knowledge to make his first Tuscan wine using Cabernet Sauvignon cuttings, from plant material originating from an old vineyard in Vecchiano (Pisa) that belonged to the family of the Dukes of Salviati. He decided to plant Cabernet because his stony soils were similar to those found in Graves, in Bordeaux. Initially the wines were solely used for home consumption, and they apparently aged very well. In the late 60s Mario sought advice from Giacomo Tachis (the most famous and inspirational Italian wine consultant) and the great Emile Peynaud (the godfather of French winemaking and the author of the only book on winemaking I have ever bought!). This prescient decision improved the quality of the wine made at this estate. The first release of Sassicaia proper came in 1968 and in the coming years the estate began to amass a following of fascinated

and faithful acolytes. I am sure that, back then, nobody could have predicted what would happen in the next decade because in 1978, the 1972 vintage of Sassicaia won a Decanter Magazine blind tasting against some massive names from Bordeaux and also some Cabernet specialists from further afield. Ironically the bottles wore the quality classification of Vino da Tavola (the lowest marque of all) on their labels, because at the time, neither D.O.C. nor D.O.C.G. existed in the Bolgheri area for red wines at all. This classification has subsequently been changed a little under intense pressure from the wine producers and collectors alike, via the largely meaningless IGT class (Indicazione geografica tipica – or rather 'tastes like where it comes from') to the new D.O.C. Bolgheri Sassicaia - the only estate in Italy that has got its kind of "private" DOC.

Nicolò Incisa della Rocchetta, son of Mario and Clarice della Gherardesca, took

over the estate from his father, after he died, in 1983. He continued to run a very tight ship, broadening the portfolio and maintaining his father's high standards. With the Antinoris as cousins (see Ornellaia) there is a quietly competitive spirit in Tuscany which has pushed the production of these exceptional Super Tuscan wines to rival the finest reds in the world. Add to this perfectionism a uniquely Italian flair and these wines are a heady concoction of glamour, integrity, nobility and a laser-guided sense of place.

02

|03

The Tenuta San Guido estate is a huge 2600ha property of which two thirds includes wild woodland at altitude and an environmental oasis nearer the coastline. Gentle hills sweep down to the Tyrrhenian Sea and the dunes from a height of 400m, and as well as the 85ha of vines there is also a stud farm for breeding the glorious Dormello Olgiata breed of racehorses. There are now three red wines made here. Le Difese, a 70% Cabernet Sauvignon, 30% Sangiovese blend has recently joined the portfolio and this is where you should start if you are to climb the Sassicaia ladder. Made to drink on release, around 10,000 cases are made each year. In 2000 a second wine was released called Guidalberto - a slightly larger production and made from a blend of 60% Cabernet Sauvignon, 40% Merlot. This wine alone is worthy of great praise such is its complexity and charm. The great wine, Sassicaia, sits on top of the portfolio and with a production of around 15,000 cases per year it is around the same output as a medium-sized Bordeaux Château. Cabernet Sauvignon is definitely the driving force variety planted here, but, Cabernet Franc is used in Sassicaia for fragrance, and Merlot and Sangiovese (Tuscany's most famous local variety) were only introduced later to the estate when they were created to develop the portfolio.

04

05

03 View of the old vineyard of "Quercione"
04 Image from the '80s that shows different phases of the
    cleaning and sterilisation of the barriques
05 Harvest in the vineyards of Tenuta San Guido

Poliziano

"Needless to say that this is the pinnacle wine from the entire region and it is as fine and regal as any Brunello di Montalcino or top Chianti."

Montepulciano
Tuscany
Established 1961

Italian Renaissance classical scholar and poet, Angelo Ambrogini (1454-1494), known as 'Il Poliziano', who was born in Montepulciano.

In 1978, Dino's son Federico decided to study agriculture in Florence which led to him taking up a post in general agriculture in the North of Italy. This experience stood him in good stead for his return home where he could apply his skills to his family wine business. Times were tough in the 80s and Federico left no stone unturned in his pursuit of perfection. This was when I first came across the wines of Poliziano and I haven't diverted my attention from this property for one single second since. Federico's relationships with consultants Carlo Ferrini and Maurizio Castelli have meant that he has surrounded himself with star talent which has rubbed off. The key to success came from his desire to capture the essence of Montepulciano coupled with modernising the viticulture and vinification sides of the businesses. Consequently, the wines immediately possessed a sense of place, all the while remaining approachable in their youth, beautifully generous, as well as detailed and complex with the ability to age.

With 30ha of vines around the winery and further plots in the greater region totalling 120ha vines in all, this is a sizeable business. Nearly half of the vineyards were planted between 1962

01 *The iconic Asinone*
02 *Poliziano's Estate*

• Dino Carletti bought a 22ha estate in 1961, in order to get in touch with the earth and the culture of his birth place of Montepulciano. From the start he set out to make top flight, handmade wines. His company took its name from the

| 02

and 1980 with the Prugnolo Gentile variety – the local name for Sangiovese. This material came from native species collected in vineyards dating from the 40s and so these old vines form the historic heart of the wines. The younger plantings include Cabernet Sauvignon, Merlot and a variety of clones of Sangiovese and another selection of Prugnolo Gentile. This diversity allows for the layering of flavour which is so prevalent in the wines from this noble estate. There are four main red wines made at Poliziano and every single one is a star. The Rosso di Montepulciano is the entry level wine made predominantly from Sangiovese with a dash of Merlot. This is a beautiful, forward, black fruit cocktail of a wine with seamless tannins and it embodies the true character of the region.

Its price tag puts it firmly in the everyday section of your wine rack which is remarkable, considering the charm and refinement on board. One step up, you find the magnificent estate wine Vino Nobile di Montepulciano. Prugnolo Gentile is the star here, with 15% Colorino, Canaiolo and Merlot in the mix. With 12-16 months aging in 20% new French oak and 80% older barriques and tonneaux, this is a wonderfully balanced wine with tension and poise on the palate and incredible distinction throughout its stunning length. I absolutely adore this wine and it alone is reason enough for this estate's inclusion in my 100, but there is more.

Vino Nobile di Montepulciano Selezione Asinone comes from the Asinone vineyard and it is only made in the best vintages. Needless to say that this is the pinnacle wine from the entire region and it is as fine and regal as any Brunello di Montalcino or top Chianti. I have only ever tasted this wine five times and yet every time it astounds me. A keeper, Asinone will last for more than a decade with ease, so you ought to let it slumber until the mighty tannins have relaxed. There is one more wine, Le Stanze, which is a Cabernet/Merlot blend and in true Super Tuscan style it sees full, new, French oak treatment. Unlike many of the super-polished wines made from international

varieties in Tuscany, Le Stanze manages to keep its feet on the ground and retain the strong characters of the region – which is the reason why it tastes so good. Federico has managed to balance modernity and authenticity so beautifully at Poliziano. His wines show the Carletti family passion for their history, culture and their unique place on Earth.

Argiano

"All of the reds come from vineyards at altitude, where cool nights and often breezy days allow the vines to 'relax and regroup' each evening, harnessing their flavours and loading complexity into the grapes during the long, slow ripening season."

Brunello di Montalcino
Tuscany
Established 1580

| 01

• There are a handful of gilt-edged wine estates in Montalcino but my favourite of all is Argiano. The wines from this exciting producer flirt with a slightly more modern style than many, while keeping their roots firmly interred in

the soils of this noble region. I favour the richness and fruit purity of these majestic Brunellos and with none of the stewed oak characteristics of many backward-looking estates; Argiano's reds are paragons of excellence. Interestingly, Argiano is thought to be where, in ancient times, a search was made to find Ara Jani, (or the legendary altar of the Roman Janus) the god of new beginnings. The name of this property and the character of the wines would seem aptly aligned.

Situated on the top of a hill, to the south-west of Montalcino, the Villa was built in the Renaissance period by the Peccis, a noble family from Siena. It has been passed down to today's owner Countess Noemi Marone Cinzano, of vermouth fame, who took on this business and its stunning estate in 1992.

In the past, renowned wine guru Giacomo Tachis (whose names pops up a few times in this book) consulted to this fine property and his aura undoubtedly still lingers, serving them well. Since Tachis retired, the hugely talented Hans Vinding-Diers has taken the helm and his enormous experience as a global, 'flying' winemaker has maintained the balance of ancient and modern. If you have never heard of the Hans before, conjure up an image of a Dane born in South Africa and brought up in Bordeaux – he is a rare talent and his impact at this estate is remarkable. One factor seems to affect flavour more than any other - the oak maturation regime used. Argiano favours a blend of two sorts, using a combination of new and once-used French barriques for the first four to six months of the wine's life, and then calming the impact of the oak flavours down a little by transferring the wine into larger Slavonian oak casks (called botti) for the next 18 months. Careful selection of ripe grapes, temperature control and this sensitive oak maturation plan enables the Argiano wines to retain wonderful, full fruit notes and heavenly succulence on the palate. It also means that they are remarkably balanced in their youth, but age extremely well, too. I am lucky enough to host a large number of fine wine tastings in the course of my wine duties and Argiano reds, with their suave flavours, are always instantly popular with my tasters. Argiano makes several different takes on the Brunello di Montalcino theme. All of the reds come from vineyards at altitude, where cool

nights and often breezy days allow the vines to 'relax and regroup' each evening, harnessing their flavours and loading complexity into the grapes during the long, slow ripening season.

Another factor which explains the consistency of the vintages at Argiano is the estate's relative proximity to Monte Amiata, one of Tuscany's highest peaks which shelters a lot of the area from the worst of the weather. The twin hallmarks of Argiano's Brunello di Montalcino are: silky tannins and generous amplitude of fruit on the palate. These are not heavy wines, but long, lithe and elegant reds with complex red and black fruit notes perfectly integrated with oak and wild herb nuances. It is the subtlety and effortless calm that makes these wines so alluring. Sangiovese can be an awkward, angular grape, but kid-glove handling transforms it into an ethereal pleasure. The Brunello's younger sibling is the

Rosso di Montalcino, also made from 100% Sangiovese, coming from the vines that encircle the winery. This is a forward-drinking red which dials back the power of the Brunello, but lacks nothing in terms of charm and complexity. So often Rossos are lean, sinewy and raw, but the Argiano version is utterly charming. Another wine made here is Non Confunditur. This is the Latin motto of the former owners, the Lovatelli Gaetani d'Aragona family, and it means 'not to be confused with', which is good advice because this delightful red, first made in 2002, is a modernist, early-drinking take on the Super Tuscan model. Made from a blend of Cabernet Sauvignon, Merlot, Syrah and Sangiovese, it is the perfect wine to introduce newcomers to the charms of Montalcino's reds, before you hit them with a pure Sangiovese. Clearly using Bordeaux grapes and a Rhône grape in the mix, covers a lot of familiar bases for one's palate.

| 03

| 04

My favourite, iconic Super Tuscan wine in Montalcino is Argiano's Solengo, meaning 'lone wild boar'. It is made from Cabernet Sauvignon, Petit Verdot, Merlot and Syrah, harvested from the finest plots of land on the property. Vinding-Diers has finessed Tachis's original Solengo project bringing élan to this wine. Rich and plush on the palate, this cuvée is a hedonistic joy. It ages like clockwork and mellows beautifully after a decade. The final great wine made at Argiano is Suolo. Invented by Vinding-Diers, Suolo is made from 100% Sangiovese grapes from two single vineyards - Vignoni, the oldest plantings from 1966 and Oliviera, planted in 1989. Suolo means 'soil' and this devastating red is a study on the exact characteristics of each exceptional plot of land. A tiny production is made each year, including 60 magnums, and I suspect that this wine will soon become one of the world's cult reds. With such an inviting list of heady red wines you must make Argiano a priority listing in your cellar.

03   *Argiano cellar*
04   *Posta L'Orciaia di Argiano, two luxury apartments, surrounded by enchanting gardens*
05   *Villa di Argiano*

Ornellaia

• Tenuta dell'Ornellaia was founded by Marchese Lodovico Antinori in 1981 and from the inaugural 1985 vintage this exceptional estate, in the stunning surroundings of Bolgheri, established itself almost overnight as one of the 'must-buy' Super Tuscans. I visited Ornellaia very early in its life and the wines were already some of the best in Italy. Today they vie not just with the Tuscan elite but the whole industry's top Bordeaux blends. In 2005 Frescobaldi bought the estate and under this new management the wines have continued to improve. In addition to Ornellaia there is a stylish Merlot made here called Masseto. This is also one of the finest Merlots in the world and certainly the top version in the country.

Planeta

"Since its inception in 1985, the Planeta winery has turned the market on its head with its pioneering dynamism."

Menfi
Sicily
Established 1985

|01

• I first tasted the wines from Planeta in the mid-90s and when I interviewed Francesca Planeta on my BBC Radio slot, she launched her brand new Santa Cecilia cuvée live on-air. It was the very first time that I had encountered a top-flight Nero d'Avola. With her Chardonnay already blowing people's minds and the estate winning the coveted Cantina dell'Anno (Italian winery of the year award in the highly respected Gambero Rosso wine guide) in 1999, Planeta was blazing an unbelievable trail. A range of stunning single varietals included a Merlot, Syrah, Cabernet Sauvignon/Franc blend called Burdese and a Fiano called Cometa which all hit the high notes. These are not only the boldest and most influential modern wines made in Sicily, but they are also among the most professional and exciting wines in the whole of Italy. Planeta simply doesn't do things by halves; their desire to innovate, while smashing rules, at the same time as celebrating indigenous varieties means that they invariably reward the drinker from the very bottom of the ladder to the top. This achievement is nothing short of breathtaking.

Since its inception in 1985, the Planeta winery has turned the market on its head with its pioneering dynamism. The Planeta cousins, Francesca, Alessio and Santi have provided the energy behind this phenomenon; mentored by Francesca's father Diego. I will never forget flying out to meet Diego Planeta and his family

02

to visit his winery, Ulmo in Sambuca di Sicilia. With over 350ha of vines at Ulmo, Dispensa in Menfi, Dorilli in Vittoria, Buonivini in Noto, Sciara Nuova in Etna and La Baronia in Capo Milazzo, they literally have the whole island covered. Diego was the most remarkable of hosts and he invited me to join him and a large group of his vineyard workers for lunch. It shouldn't have surprised me when it turned out that his guest chef was none other than Cheong Liew. Cheong worked at the Hilton in Adelaide at the time, and he is a friend of mine, not least because I always frequented his restaurant every time I travelled Down Under. Widely regarded as the father of 'fusion food' and the driving force behind contemporary Australian cuisine, it was mind-blowing to find him orchestrating the weirdest lunch that these farmers would ever eat - spiked with his zany spices and cooked in an upturned dustbin lid (an instant wok!), in the middle of the Sicilian outback. We were both struck dumb, but with typical aplomb Diego just smiled and asked me who I expected to be cooking at his winery, as if it was the most normal thing in the world.

I suppose that this story illustrates just how open-minded and unpredictable this family is. To the Planetas, everything is possible and indeed the wines show this to be true. In addition to the various flagship wines that I have already mentioned, all of which you should taste, Planeta also makes a sensational Moscato di Noto – one of Italy's most notable sweeties. The two entry level wines La Segreta Bianco and La Segreta Rosso are certainly not 'secrets' anymore because they are seen on the smartest dining room tables in the world. With 17 generations of experience, it is not surprising that there is some expertise in the field of local varieties and Grecanico, Carricante, Moscato di Noto, Fiano, Frappato, Nerello Mascalese and Nero d'Avola all feature in the portfolio. In addition to their lovely wines there is the beautiful extra virgin olive oil made at their Capparrina estate, near the beaches of Menfi. A new press facility was built in 2003 and with nearly 100ha of groves, this is a very serious operation, too.

01 *Planeta Merlot*
02 *Planeta vineyard near Mount Etna*

Obsessive about entertaining, the new boutique hotel La Foresteria, in Menfi overlooking the vineyards, is probably the best place to explore the historic Sicilian countryside, drink their cosmic wines, enjoy their celestial food and immerse yourself in the heavenly Planeta way of life.

03   *The Etna vineyard*
04   *Alessio, Francesca and Santi Planeta*
05   *Vineyards in Noto (Unesco Heritage)*

Hungary

Oremus

"If you would like to join the ranks of Peter the Great, Voltaire, Queen Victoria, Bram Stoker, Joseph Haydn, Liszt and Beethoven by becoming a Tokaj fan, you cannot do better than choosing Oremus."

Tokaj
Established 1616 / 1991

| 01

01 *Bottles of Tokaj sweet wine with the characteristic golden colour*
02 *The landscaped designer stone winery*

• I am a massive fan of Hungarian Tokaj, but I don't drink it very often and usually find that half a glass is enough because of its intensity and palate-satiating qualities. That was until I came across the wines of Oremus.

In 1616, Prince György Rákóczi I bought the Oremus vineyards which remained in this family until 1711. During this period Maté Szepsi Lackó, a Calvinist preacher, made Tokaj Aszú, for the first time, using botrytis-affected grapes as a present for Princess Zsuzsanna, György's wife. In the 18th century, the wines of Tokaj were enjoyed as far afield as Vienna, Prague, London and St Petersburg. Since then, the Oremus vineyards have been through massive upheavals including phylloxera and fragmentation of the vineyards themselves. In 1991 the Álvarez family, owners of the most revered of all Spanish wine estates, Vega Sicilia (q.v.), started discussions with the Hungarian government. Two years later Vega Sicilia founded Tokaj Oremus. Pablo Álvarez studied the history and wines of the region in great detail and, the revival of the estate and the wines started in earnest. With immense respect for the traditions and the laborious winemaking processes, the sole objective of this impassioned man has been to restore the vineyard to its former 17th and 18th century grandeur. Tokaj Oremus is located in Tolcsva, one of the most well-known villages of the Tokaj-Hegyalja region, in the northeast of Hungary. The property has 115ha of vines and both the dry and sweet wines are utterly scintillating. Mandolas, the dry wine, is made from the Furmint grape and it is aged for a brief period in Hungarian oak barrels. Oremus was the first producer to use the Furmint variety for dry wines and the result is sensational. With touches of orange blossom and lime and a freshness which lifts the palate, it is a very special creation indeed. The key to this wine is the stunningly rapier sharp acidity also found in the epic sweet wines of Oremus, too. The Late Harvest wine is made with bunches selected at the end of the picking season including 40% of aszú grapes, affected with noble rot. With six months of barrel aging, this is a lighter style of sweet wine and one that acts as the perfect springboard between the Oremus dry style and the range of Tokaj proper.

Tokaj itself is made in a time-honoured and incredibly labour-intensive manner. Aszú grapes are hand-picked one by one and collected in vats whereupon they are crushed to make a paste. Grape must is then added to the extremely sweet paste of different intensity levels called puttonyos. Three puttonyos is moderately sweet (in the scheme of things!) and the scale rises to 6 puttonyos which is very sweet indeed. The wine containing the pre-determined level of puttonyos sweetness is then fermented and matured very slowly in oak barrels. There is also one more level of Tokaj above the 6 puttonyos level called Ezsencia, which is made from the free run juice which exudes from the aszú-affected grapes. The alcohol level never rises above 6% in this wine because of the massive level of sweetness and the fermentation itself could take up to four years to

| 02

complete. The sugar levels are somewhere between 500-700g/l, so it is the sweetest of all styles of wine in the world. Not surprisingly these wines last for centuries. All of the Oremus Tokaj are luscious, pure and exceptionally well made, but it is the bright acidity and golden thread of freshness which sets them apart from other wines and also refreshes the palate after every sip. Typically served in 50cl bottles, Tokaj can conceivably serve a dinner party of eight guests! If you would like to join the ranks of Peter the Great, Voltaire, Queen Victoria, Bram Stoker, Joseph Haydn, Liszt and Beethoven by becoming a Tokaj fan, you cannot do better than choosing Oremus.

South Africa

The Sadie Family Wines

"Eben's brand, Sadie Family Wines, is certainly the 'youngest' in this book, but his inclusion is thoroughly deserved. While his wines might not be extremely well-known all over the world, there is no doubt that they are truly world-class."

Malmesbury
Swartland
Established 1999

| 01

01   *The signature wine: Columella*
02   *Old bushvines in the Paardeberg*
      Mountain

• Eben Sadie looks like a rock star, but he is nothing of the sort. He is, in fact, something much more elemental and exciting - a wine creator/philosopher/ surfer. In addition to this he is South Africa's most beguilingly talented man of wine. I use this term because he literally

does everything involved in creating his wines from the vineyard to the sales, so the term winemaker doesn't really do him justice. Sadie started his career working for Charles Back's Spice Route brand but left to pursue his own rather outlandish dreams in 1999. I have tracked his career at every stage and have even had the privilege of several scoops along the way. I have been honoured to respond to his eager questions about his wines in order to slake his thirst for debate. He makes his wines because he loves them himself; he knows they're good and that they will always find a home – more often than not within the first few days of release, such is his cult status. His wines qualify for truly gastronomic enlightenment. Each and every time I have been shocked by the flair and complexity he brings to the glass. Eben's brand, Sadie Family Wines, is certainly the 'youngest' in this book, but his inclusion is thoroughly deserved. While his wines might not be extremely well-known all over the world, there is no doubt that they are truly world-class. With very small production, the wines are all highly sought-after and I have a feeling that as South Africa continues on its trajectory of improving its fine wine offering year on year, Sadie Family Wines will gain legions more fans.

Based in Malmesbury, in the Swartland region, Sadie makes wines from old parcels of fruit and his brilliant releases need to be tasted to be believed. Favouring blends rather than single varietals, he understands that Swartland is suited to complex aromatic whites and reds and so he draws parallels between his own region, the Rhône Valley and the Mediterranean. His most important red wine, Columella, is named after Lucius Junius Moderatus Columella the author of De Re Rustica, a 12-volume masterpiece expounding the virtues of agricultural practices in the Roman empire. Columella is a Shiraz/Mourvèdre/ Grenache blend with staggering earth, fynbos (indigenous scrub and heath land vegetation) and game notes. This is not a blockbuster as such; preferring to pack the palate with intrigue rather than brawn and it is an experience worth hunting down. The other star in his two-wine constellation is Palladius, named after another Roman agriculture author. Palladius is a white blend that follows a Rhône model but that utilises as many as eight varieties. Chenin Blanc is often involved not least because it is South Africa's most exciting white grape. Eben has tracked down ancient vineyards from which he draws his fruit,

some of which were abandoned and overgrown. Grenache Blanc, Clairette, Viognier and Chardonnay also bring their own special nuances to the finished wine.

Two Sequillo wines, a red and a white, are made by Sadie in a joint venture with Cornel Spies. Meaning 'an arid, dry place of great purity', Sequillo wines are often seen as second wines to Columella and Palladius. They are in fact distinctly different even though they are made using a broadly similar philosophy. The white blend uses Palomino, Clairette Chenin Blanc, Semillon, Grenache Blanc, Semillon Gris and Viognier while the red sticks to a more familiar palette of Syrah, Mourvèdre, Grenache, Carignan and Cinsault. These are both immensely satisfying and superb value wines. Sadie also makes a serious Priorat in Spain, called Dits Del Terra – this is another of the most exceptional wines that I have tasted from the region and it explains his fascination and obsession with earthy,

honest, mighty and mercurial blends. If you haven't already introduced your palate to Eben's wines then do so without delay – the pleasure will be all yours!

Rustenberg

"If you haven't been to South Africa, then this winery is a decent reason to get on the plane."

Stellenbosch
Established 1682

RUSTENBERG

Stellenbosch Chardonnay

| 01

• Rustenberg is one of the most beautiful wine farms in the Cape. Sitting at the foot of the Simonsberg Mountain, close to South Africa's wine nerve centre of Stellenbosch, this is a crucial destination for avid wine fans and an important working farm too. Showcasing the symmetry and grandeur of Cape Dutch architecture, this imposing property oozes class. Established in 1682, and producing some 3,000 cases of wine annually by 1781, it became a fast growing, renowned winery well over a century ago. Wine has been bottled at the cellar since 1892, which is staggering considering that estate bottling in Burgundy didn't occur for another 30 years. It was also in this year that John X Merriman rescued the estate after a period of recession and decline. Immortalised on a wine label today, John X also went on to become Prime Minister of the Cape. Peter Barlow bought the estate in 1941; his son Simon took over in 1987 perpetuating Rustenberg's ongoing success. Recent times have seen the charismatic winemaker Adi Badenhorst lead and launch the wines into the modern wine-drinkers' consciousness before the talented Randolph Christians, Adi's second-in-command took over the top job.

Since then the wines have taken on a cool, calm and suave air. Remarkably, the Rustenberg wine portfolio displays grounded restraint deep at the core of every wine. A crisp Sauvignon Blanc, with tense, focused lime juice fruit and flashes of exotic flavours; an unwooded

Chardonnay which shares more similarities with a fine Chablis than most South African versions of this variety and, two spectacular oaked Chardonnays lead the way. The estate version is widely available, eminently affordable and one of the most reliably delicious in the Cape - treated to smart French oak and made from the same recipe as all top white Burgundies, it is a star wine. The top Chardonnay cuvée is called Five Soldiers, and has a much more structured style with weight, depth of fruit and complexity. This is one of the Cape's finest white wines. Not content with classic white varieties made in the time-honoured fashion, there is the racy Roussanne as well as a challenging white blend made from Viognier, Semillon and Roussanne, called Schoongezicht.

The reds at Rustenberg tend not to be too extracted or oaky and in this respect they are modelled on a European chassis and appeal to a wide range of connoisseurs. The Syrah is dark purple, lusty and yet not too ripe or port-like. RM Nicholson, named after Reg Merriman Nicholson, a former owner and winemaker who lived at Rustenberg for 30 years, is a complex blend of Cabernet Sauvignon, Syrah, Petit Verdot, Cabernet Franc and Malbec. Light in tannin despite heavyweight ingredients, the skill that Randolph shows here is in the art of blending and layering the fruit flavours. It is a sensual experience and one which harks back to a previous age when a 'Dry Red' estate wine was made following an old fashioned shove-it-all-in-together recipe. John X Merriman is the most famous red cuvée here and it is a classic 'Bordeaux blend' utilising all five classic varieties - Cabernet Sauvignon, Merlot, Petit Verdot, Cabernet Franc and Malbec. I adore this wine, not least because of its build-quality /price tag ratio – this wine is exceptional

value and you must track it down. Climbing up the ladder, you come to the wine named after Peter Barlow himself. Made from 100% Cabernet Sauvignon, this is the icon wine at Rustenberg; a beautifully lush and densely packed blackcurrant creation with a 20-year lifespan perfect for true collectors. The portfolio also extends to a cunning Straw Wine made from Chenin Blanc; a luscious, sweet, exotic treat. All of the

wines made here reflect the distinguished, historic Rustenberg estate. If you haven't been to South Africa, then this winery is a decent reason to get on the plane.

01   Rustenburg Stellenbosch Chardonnay
02   Simonsberg Mountain overlooking vineyards

| 02

Franschhoek | *Boekenhoutskloof*

• Marc Kent's winemaking at Boekenhoutskloof is exemplary. If you cannot pronounce the name you will definitely recognise the seven chairs on the label. Marc makes everything from entry level Porcupine Ridge supermarket wines, via a brilliant Wolftrap red, rosé and white trio, to everyone's favourite The Chocolate Block, a complex red blend and finally to South Africa's finest red wine (his Syrah) and its stable mates. He never fails to thrill the palate. His passion and manic obsession with trying anything to improve his stellar creations year after year is to be greatly respected. A superbly leesy, limey and dry Semillon kicks off the Boekenhoutskloof range. We then pass to a chiselled and honed Cabernet and my favourite wine, the staggeringly complex and 'moreish' Syrah. There is one other wine, a sort of secret project, called Journeyman. This Cabernet Franc-dominant wine is so sought-after I expect I will receive a knock at the door for even mentioning it in this book, so shhh.

Australia

Cullen Wines

"Certainly one of the most beautiful Australian Cabernets I have ever tasted, as well as being the equal of any of the Left Bank Bordeaux of the same vintage."

Margaret River
Western Australia
Established 1966

• I will never forget getting up very early one morning and walking up and down the rows of vines at Cullen, tasting grapes to check their ripeness with winemaker Vanya Cullen, and then wandering back to the winery to enjoy breakfast with her and her mother Di. During breakfast Di opened a bottle of her 1986 Cabernet – it was utterly sensational and certainly one of the most beautiful Australian Cabernets I have ever tasted, as well as being the equal of any of the Left Bank Bordeaux of the same vintage. I sensed that I was in the presence of a magnificent lady and I was extremely grateful to have had the chance to spend some time with her before she passed away in 2003. Diana Madeline Cabernet is the estate's flagship wine and Di's husband Kevin, who died in 1994, is also remembered with Cullen Wines' Kevin John Chardonnay. Both wines are among the greatest wines in the country and it is fitting that we are reminded of them often because they - along with a handful of other families - were pioneers in the world famous Margaret River region of Western Australia.

Eminent agronomist Dr John Gladstone's studies of the region drew parallels between the climate of Margaret River and Bordeaux. This encouraged Dr. Kevin and Diana Cullen to plant a trial acre of vines at Wilyabrup (a place I call 'Aussie Pauillac' for obvious reasons) in, the heart of Margaret River, in 1966. They were impressed with the performance of their

vines and this encouraged them to plant a further 18 acres of vines on their sheep and cattle farm in 1971. While Kevin worked his day job as a doctor, Di managed the winery and became chief winemaker in 1981. A year later, she made history by becoming the first woman to win a Trophy at the Perth Royal Show. In 1983 she was joined by her daughter Vanya, who was later made chief winemaker in 1989. It is no overstatement to say that this staggeringly talented, brave family has inspired an entire wine industry in Margaret River and beyond, in greater Western Australia. Both Kevin and Di were awarded the Member for the Order of Australia – Kevin for medicine and wine and Di for viticulture and wine – among many other accolades.

Today the estate is certified biodynamic, carbon neutral and naturally powered and the wine range is finer than ever. Vanya is regarded as one of the most talented winemakers in the country and also one of the most acute tasters on the judging circuit. Her wines are sold on allocation in all

corners of the globe and Diana Madeline Cabernet is one of only 17 wines in the 'Outstanding' category of the Langtons Classification.

None of the Cullen wines have yeast additions, acid additions or use malolactic culture. The Cullen mantra is that they are totally natural wines which express the place and land on which they are grown, the vintage and the people who make them. I can tell you that they wholly achieve their aim. The experience you encounter when you drink Cullen wines is unlike any other. I never rush the wines themselves whether it is the more forward Margaret River Red, the Mangan Vineyard range or the flagship styles. These are wines that demand to be cogitated, adored and savoured. My picks of the range include the devastatingly complex Mangan Vineyard Sauvignon Blanc/Semillon – a wine that sits around the 12% alc. vol. mark and utilises around 20% new oak to add padding to its belly, but which still pulverises the taste buds with raspingly pure lime juice notes. Kevin

01 *Diana and Kevin*
02 *Tending the vines*

John Chardonnay is a wine that I never seem to order enough of. It has made my 100 Best Australian Wines list on numerous occasions and, more often than not, at some of my Australian masterclasses, I hear people whispering that it is the finest Aussie Chardonnay that they have ever tasted (and that includes all of the competition!). Mangan Malbec/Petit Verdot/Merlot is less of an obvious crowd-pleaser and more of a conundrum. With a heavenly scent of wild flowers and mulberries, this somewhat unusual blend always appeals to quirky palates and I have to confess that I adore its unconventional aromas and eclectic charm. Finally you have Diana Madeline, the most incredible Cabernet Sauvignon-based wine in the region, which involves Malbec, Cabernet Franc, Petit Verdot and Merlot in the mix depending on the vintage. There is a regal note to this wine which is truly awe-inspiring and just one sip will make you realise exactly why Di and Kevin took the plunge to plant the vineyard over 40 years ago.

03

04

03   *Plunging red fermentation tank*
04   *Chardonnay vines at dusk*
05   *Vanya Cullen*

Leeuwin Estate

• Denis and Tricia Horgan set up Leeuwin, in the idyllic surroundings of Margaret River, in the early '70s. Rather than using just any old wine consultant they availed themselves of the services of the legendary Californian wine hero Robert Mondavi. Clearly the decisions made 40 years ago were the right ones because Leeuwin makes world class wines and certainly my favourite Chardonnay in the country. I have tasted every vintage of Art Series Chardonnay, their iconic flagship wine labelled with a piece of indigenous Australian art each release, since 1983. Every single wine has been a joy and Prelude, the second label, is also a stunning release. They also make sterling Cabernet, Sauvignon Blanc and Riesling. The concerts in the grounds are spectacular, too.

Clare Valley
South Australia

Jim Barry

• Jim Barry, the first qualified winemaker to work in the Clare back in 1959, is an institution in the region. Since Jim's death in 2004, his son Peter has, with the help of his sons Sam and Tom, run the winery which, given its geographical location, is a Shiraz, Cabernet and Riesling specialist. Their iconic flagship wine, The Armagh Shiraz comes from a vineyard planted by Jim in 1968 and to which I awarded a perfect score for the 2006 vintage. Benbournie is a stunning Cabernet Sauvignon that is wild and untamed. 'Pb' (named after Peter Barry himself) is a mesmerising Shiraz / Cabernet blend.

With The Lodge Hill Dry Riesling and Shiraz - two of Australia's most over-delivering, every-day priced wines - you already have a captivating portfolio. Their most important white wine is The Florita Riesling, a minute production from a sensational single vineyard that brings a tear to the eye such is its pristine minerality and poise.

Grosset

"His brand is as highly recognised and awarded as any in Australia but his humility and work ethic are second to none, and this is what makes him so endearing. This is one iconic estate that demonstrates one man's genius crystal-clearly in every glass."

Clare Valley
South Australia
Established 1981

• Grosset Wines is located in Auburn at the Southern End of the Clare Valley, about 100 kilometres north of Adelaide in South Australia. The Clare Valley is a Mecca for lovers of dry, prickly, lime juice-imbued Riesling and savoury, swarthy, enigmatic red wines made predominantly from Shiraz and Cabernet. It is this region which fashions the most seductive and age-worthy of all Australian dry Rieslings and Grosset Wines is the most famous name around.

Established in 1981 by the eponymous Jeffrey Grosset, it's a true boutique winery making several different labels, but with a maximum production of only 12,000 cases, it's similar in size and output to a small, top-flight Burgundy Domaine. With four main sources of fruit - three in Clare and one in the Adelaide Hills - this is a multi-skilled operation which excels at a challenging range of vinous disciplines. Jeff is one of the most inspirational men I have ever met; he is highly engaging and very generous with his time and knowledge. He has inspired legions of young Aussie winemakers to strive for perfection and his stance on screw caps is legendary. He and a few other pioneers in Clare were the first to take this innovative closure on well over a decade ago and well before the Marlborough Sauvignon Blanc gang got there!

Over the last 10 years his passion and scientific understanding in trusting his wines to this type of closure has led

to virtually every other serious winery in the world trialling, if not using, this closure. Jeff's wines are utterly sublime and appear on the most discerning wine lists in the world. If someone says to you 'Clare Riesling', the most famous name to always crop up is Jeff's. There are two main Rieslings in his portfolio - Springvale Watervale Riesling and Polish Hill Riesling. Springvale is found on high ground in the north-eastern corner of the Watervale sub-region. The topsoil is rich and red over limestone; the vines are robust, laden with generous fruit which parades piercingly forward, precocious characteristics.

By comparison, Springvale always seems to be earlier drinking than Polish Hill, but this is an illusion. Springvale is immediately pleasing, requires less concentration and yet ages with grace and persistence, along a differing but no less noble trajectory than Polish Hill. It has an energy about it which seems innocent, unsullied and delicate. Polish Hill however is more brutal terrain, sitting in a U-shaped ridge north

of Mount Horrocks, with smaller vines, smaller bunches and where a harder-working attitude abounds. The wine is firm, savoury, mineral-soaked, often closed in its youth and certainly more intense than its stable mate. In some vintages it flatters to deceive, but always reveals its hand after five or so years. Perfect depictions of the two moods of Clare Valley Riesling. Lazy wine lovers need look no further than this estate to experience a range (albeit of two) flavours. Keen oenophiles can look as hard as they like for others but these two wines will feature in every top Clare selection. Both are reliable' consistently stunning and both epitomise Clare. The masculine and feminine, the 'drink now' and the 'put in the cellar', the lighter soil and the heavier soil – you cannot predict which wine you'll prefer in any one vintage so you need to collect both every year!

Jeff also has an exceptional Clare Valley red wine called Gaia. A blend of Cabernet Sauvignon and Cabernet Franc, it comes from an amazing single vineyard in the

middle of corn fields 570m above the Valley. It is as mesmerising and elemental as any red I have ever tasted - I love it because it's as raw and unspoilt as the wild Valley itself. Jeff also switches codes to include a Semillon/Sauvignon Blanc that segues between two wine regions – the Semillon slice is from the Clare Valley and the Sauvignon Blanc part hails from the Adelaide Hills.

01   *Grosset's Polish Hill Riesling*
02   *Grosset vineyard*

| 03

The theory is that he draws on the prime territory for each of the two grapes and this in turn lends an extra dimension of complexity to the finished article. Another critically acclaimed wine, it is essential drinking and a rich, bold and marvellous counterpoint to single varietals from other wineries from either region. His Chardonnay comes from the beautiful Piccadilly Valley in the Adelaide Hills and it is always a profound joy. The sensitivity of oak in this fairly robust wine is perfectly judged and it certainly shows why Australian Chardonnay is among the finest category of white wines in the world. The two final wines are - a sultry, sensual Adelaide Hills Pinot Noir that makes the most of its briary, earthy notes and one of only a handful of top-flight Pinots still

made in the Hills and, secondly, an Off-Dry Clare Riesling which has caught the eye of restaurateurs chasing the more familiar Northern European model. The fashion for juicy, touch-of-grapiness Rieslings is gathering momentum in Australia and New Zealand and if Riesling is on the agenda Grosset's name is sure to be in the mix. There is no doubt that Jeff is a Clare Valley specialist, but his results in the Adelaide Hills are astounding too. His brand is as highly recognised and awarded as any in Australia but his humility and work ethic are second to none, and this is what makes him so endearing. This is one iconic estate that demonstrates one man's genius crystal-clearly in every glass.

| 04

| 05

Peter Lehmann

"The archetypal Australian: big, vocal, funny and forthright but also a clever communicator and an outstanding promoter of all Australian wines."

Barossa Valley
South Australia
Established 1979

• Peter Lehmann is arguably the most famous man in the Australian wine business. His eponymous brand has possibly had more impact on wine lovers and the wine trade than any other living Aussie. A Member of the Order of Australia in the inaugural list of Australian Honours for his contribution to Australian wine; he was the first Australian wine industry figure to be recognised in this way.

My memories of Peter go back 25 years when I would meet him in London during his trips over to promote his wines. I had never met anyone like him in my life. He's the archetypal Australian: big, vocal, funny and forthright but also a clever communicator and an outstanding promoter of all Australian wines.

The story of how he got to London and enchanted the international markets is a fascinating one indeed. Peter is Barossan through and through having fought for his region, his growers and his wines for over 65 years. Starting out in the wine business at the tender age of 17; his first job was working for the great Rudi Kronberger at Yalumba, where in 1959 his capacity to learn fast earned him the role of winemaker and manager of Saltram Wines. During his 20 years there he created Mamre Brook, the company's flagship wine, in 1963, and gained admiration for his top quality, authentic yet 'modern' Barossa wines. Some of his Shirazes from the 1960s are regarded as the finest examples of this grape made in Australia – many still drinking perfectly today and setting a global benchmark for this variety. While presiding over Saltram, Peter increased production from 400 tonnes to more than 6,000. Such was his trustworthiness and honesty that a vast number of independent grape growers supplied Saltram without any contract. Peter's word was his bond – a dictum more recently used for one of the Lehmann wine ranges.

In 1976 Peter was joined at Saltram by Andrew Wigan and while Peter has now retired, 'Wigs' (Wigan) still works at full pelt assisted by a remarkable team, and he has been involved with every single Peter Lehmann wine since '76. In 1978, a huge grape surplus across Australia prompted Saltram's owners to instruct Peter to renege on his agreements with his grape growers. Peter refused to do so however; he knew that most of his growers would subsequently lose everything they had spent their lives building. With the financial backing of family and friends Peter created a new company called Masterson to buy all of the growers' grapes and found finance to build a new winery just in time for the 1980 vintage.

His investors took principal ownership of the company with Peter a minority shareholder. He has survived some great financial scrapes in his time and the fact that the wines only ever improved year-on-year is testament to his acumen, his winery staff and their consummate skill. When his principal shareholder pulled the plug in 1983 Peter took a second gamble. This time he offered equity in the company via a public float. Fittingly, the growers he had stood by in the past and the fervently loyal staff all pitched in to invest in the new business along with thousands of smaller investors, raising money in record time. Peter's last major roll of the dice came in 2003 fighting off an aggressive takeover bid from the multinational drinks corporation, Allied Domecq. I remember having dinner at his home with him and his wife Margaret during

this period and he wasn't quite his normal self. Yet he remained effortlessly charming, and having recently dined with the Queen and President Clinton, (at separate events) touchingly said it was me he'd been looking forward to seeing that week. Opposed to the Allied Domecq takeover idea, he went on to select the Hess Group as his favoured partner valiantly battling to secure Lehmann's ongoing stake in the company. When I spoke to him shortly after the deal went through he said he felt: "Bleeping rich" (for the first time in his life) and that he was looking forward to going fishing. This consummate gambler went to the table three times and won each time.

01 *Lehmann's iconic Stonewell Shiraz.*
02 *Cellar Door in the Barossa Valley.*

| 02

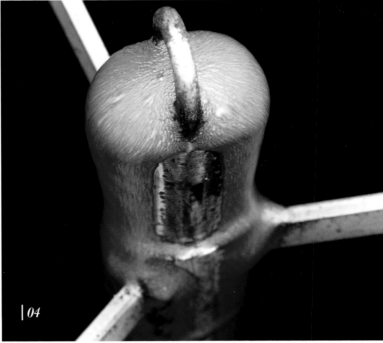

Morally he was right every time, but how often does that help you in business? We are, of course, the beneficiaries of his loyalty and graft. Peter Lehmann wines has over 150 growers, the business has been through a recent label makeover and times are good. Andrew Wigan's name appears on the old Reserve Riesling label now and he has numerous awards to his name. As one of Australia's most successful winemakers, he was named Gourmet Traveller Wine Magazine's Winemaker of the Year in 2009, White Winemaker of the Year at the International Wine Challenge in 2006 and the International Wine and Spirit Competition's International Winemaker of the Year in 2003 and 2006. Along the way, he has won numerous trophies including

the Jimmy Watson. His proudest wine is the 1993 Reserve Riesling. Not surprising, as it went on to win 32 trophies and 47 gold medals around the world; arguably the most successful show white wine in Australian wine show history.

In 1987 Peter and Wigs created the first Stonewell Shiraz from specially selected parcels of fruit and the best barrels. I scored the 2004 Stonewell 20/20 in my notes – a rare perfect wine. It is categorically one of the best value Shiraz on the planet that you simply must taste. The Peter Lehmann Masters Series includes the aforementioned Wigan Riesling, Margaret Semillon (after Peter's wife), Eight Songs Shiraz, Mentor Cabernet and

a botrytised Semillon – all of which are sensational, unmissable wines. They sing of the Barossa and Eden Valley regions which Peter has spent his life championing. Along with a vast range of everyday wines and restaurant labels, Peter Lehmann is a name you can trust – but you know that already.

03 *Row 8 from the revered Stonewell vineyard.*
04 *Fermenting another parcel of premium Barossa Shiraz.*
05 *One of the many PLW grower's vineyards dotted across the length and breadth of the Barossa Valley.*

Penfolds

"Today Penfolds' portfolio is diverse and while the emphasis has always been on mighty, age-worthy red wines, the whites pick up as many trophies in wine shows as the reds."

Barossa Valley
South Australia
Established 1844

A trio of great Penfolds wines

| 01 | *A trio of great Penfolds wines* |
| 02 | *A Cellar at the historic and heritage protected Penfolds Magill Estate in Adelaide* |

• You might have expected Penfolds to feature in this celestial century of estates because it is the proud maker of Australia's most revered red wine - Grange, a mighty Shiraz, often made with a dribble of Cabernet in the blend for good measure. However, it's crucial to note that this incredible company is an awful lot more than a one trick pony. You have to travel back a long way to unravel the story of Penfolds and its English founder, Dr Christopher Rawson Penfold, who was born in 1811. Penfold studied medicine at St Bartholomew's Hospital in London graduating in 1838. Six years later he set sail for Australia with his wife Mary where they bought the Mackgill estate (later changed to Magill) living in the homestead they called Grange. At the time, Penfolds produced a fortified wine tonic, for patients with anaemia, made from Grenache cuttings from the Southern Rhône. Following on from her husband's death, Mary Penfold assumed the running of the company in 1870 and became a formidable wine matriarch.

A catalogue from 1889 lists the wines that came from the Grange and Magill vineyards as 'Mataro, Grenache, Constantia, Grange Port, Frontignac, Grange Tawny, Pedro Ximenes (sic), Tokay, Madeira, Grange Sherry and Muscadine' – quite a line up and exactly the sort of wine list that I would be very happy to browse today. When Mary's daughter Georgina and son-in-law Thomas Hyland took over, they created Penfolds and Co. and by the time Mary passed away in 1896, the company was producing over one third of South Australia's wine.

From 1943 onwards throughout the decade, Penfolds acquired a number of

vineyards and wineries, namely Auldana and Kalimna; gradually shifting from fortified wines to table wines to suit the modern palate. Penfolds' chief winemaker, the legendary Max Schubert, went on to create Australia's most famous wine, Grange Hermitage in 1951 which was then commercially released in 1953. Later it became Grange, the country's foremost structured red wine.

It's impressive to note that many of that period's original wines are still widely drunk today. Penfolds and Co. went public in 1962 with the Penfold family retaining a controlling interest until 1976. During these years the Bin Series of red wines was developed by Max Schubert passing through the hands of Don Ditter in '76, John Duval in '86 and Peter Gago from 2002 to present day. The Yattarna Chardonnay project (nicknamed White Grange) was started and RWT (red wine trial) was introduced to provide a counterpoint Shiraz to Grange, using exclusively French oak as opposed to American. The 2004 vintage saw the release of Block 42, an incredible Kalimna Cabernet, as well as Bin 60A a Cabernet/ Shiraz blend. It copied the first vintage of this wine, the fabulous 1962 – which is the single most awarded wine in Australia's wine show history. In 2008, Gago created the iconic Bin 620, a Coonawarra Cabernet/ Shiraz – the first one since Max Schubert made an experimental version of this blend in 1966. I have tasted this wine on several occasions and it is sublime. In 2010

Penfolds introduced their first Bin 23 Pinot Noir, proving that this eminent house is not just a Cabernet and Shiraz specialist. These days, Penfolds' fame is truly international with Peter racking up more air miles than any other winemaker I know.

The Penfolds re-corking clinics have become institutions, too. You are invited to bring old bottles of Penfolds wines to these events for assessment, as well as topping up and recorking if they are ullaged. Peter tells of a story where an old lady in Hobart, Tasmania, came along to have her wines assessed and she was sure that she had an untouched case of the

phenomenal 1953 Grange, still in its straw wrapping. Gago said to her that it wasn't 1953 Grange Hermitage and for a moment her face dropped, before he told her that it was in fact the ultra-rare 1953 Grange Cabernet – a tiny release in that vintage. This contact with the consumer, collector and fan, is unique and it further cements the relationship between this amazing wine estate and its supporters. Today Penfolds' portfolio is diverse and while the emphasis has always been on mighty, age-worthy red wines, the whites (in particular the Chardonnays with Yattarna at the top of the pile and the Reserve Bin A - an exclusively Adelaide Hills-based wine) pick up as many

|03

|04

|05

trophies in wine shows as the reds. You can still drink Penfolds wines at everyday prices, too. The recently re-released Koonunga Hill Seventy Six Shiraz Cabernet is a steal and it echoes the style and bravado of a bygone era. My personal favourite in the red wine collection is St Henri Shiraz – for me it is a more approachable Grange-style offering, made with no new oak whatsoever. I am lucky enough to go behind the scenes at Penfolds every year and taste unreleased wines, and I can assure you that this is one company which never stops thinking about refining and evolving its offering. Penfolds started off a heroic ascendancy into the world of fine wine with Grange, but the phenomenal, diverse portfolio is just as exciting and it is this which entrances the masses in the hope that they, too, one day, will taste the iconic Grange. In particular, look out for the 2006 – it got a perfect 20/20 in my 100 Best Australian Wines notes.

01   *Penfolds Block 42 Vines, the oldest plantings of continuously produced Cabernet in the world*

02   *Penfolds barrels at the Magill Estate*

03   *Large old wooden Vats at Penfolds. This traditional approach allows the wine to develop, imparting minimal oak character as with the Penfolds St. Henri*

Tyrrell's

"Each Tyrrell generation has favoured and championed a different grape – Edward loved Shiraz, Murray pioneered Chardonnay and Murray's son Bruce who joined the company in 1974 is a great fan of Semillon."

Hunter Valley
New South Wales
Established 1858

| 01

01   *New 2,500 litre French oak barrel for Hunter Shiraz maturation*

02   *Chardonnay Vines on the Short Flat vineyard looking up to the Brokenback range*

• In 2008, Tyrrell's celebrated its 150th anniversary of making wine in the Hunter Valley. It was one and a half centuries and five generations ago that Edward Tyrrell arrived in Pokolbin. Today, it's Bruce Tyrrell, the most renowned exponent of dry Semillon on the planet who's taken on the role of company patriarch. To understand the family history, it's the early days of Edward and his offspring that reveal the single-minded vision, pioneering determination and outspoken attitude responsible for some of the most scintillating wines imaginable.

In 1854, Edward Tyrrell left England for Sydney, Australia where he bought 320 acres of prime Hunter Valley land, flanking the Brokenback Range. Initially, he was disappointed with his lot. His was one of the last remaining properties for sale in the area, which seemingly lacked the fertility of the river soils so prized for cattle farming and also flourishing vineyards. He decided to plant the land with vine cuttings propagated from the famous James Busby plant material imported from Europe in 1832, focusing on Shiraz and Semillon. He built his first home there with his own hands in 1858; followed by a winery in 1863 yielding his first wine a year later. His marriage to Susan Hungerford in 1869 was the dawn of a phenomenal Australian vinous dynasty. The eldest of their 10 children, also named Edward (but called Dan) followed in his father's footsteps creating his first vintage in 1889. He became great friends with Maurice O'Shea and Leo Buring. When Edward died in 1909 it was discovered that his choice of properties was actually the luckiest of all; boasting some of the finest limestone soils in the region. His youngest son, Avery soon took over the vineyards, thereby cementing the property's reputation with the help of his sibling, Dan.

Avery's outspoken son Murray then took over in 1959, as part of the third generation, whose straightforward mantra was: 'Once you add anything to wine, you never improve it'. With the wine industry of the day in decline, Murray opted to focus solely on their top wines. The Private Bin initiative started with individual wines matured in numbered 2250-litre casks. Visitors would taste the wines directly from the vats before placing their orders for these unique wines unavailable elsewhere. People would travel miles for the experience; fuelling the thriving tourist industry that ensued as well as the Private Bin Club, Australia's first mail order club. Vat 1 Semillon, Vat 6 Pinot Noir, Vat 8 Shiraz/Cabernet, Vat 9 Shiraz and Vat 47 Chardonnay are the surviving wines from this era and the flagship Tyrrell cuvées of today.

Murray shared a love of white Burgundy with his great friend Len Evans - a wine legend in his own right. During this period of the 60s, Chardonnay was virtually unheard of, and yet Penfolds had some in their HVD (Hunter Valley Distillery) vineyard. Murray was aware of its existence from childhood memories of eating bunches of it, so when his request for some cuttings was turned down, he naturally felt compelled to make his famous 'Midnight Leap' over the fence to 'liberate' some Chardonnay material. Tyrrell's first Chardonnay was made in 1969 and it was the first to be commercially released in Australia followed by Vat 47 in 1971. These days Chardonnay accounts for a staggering 18% of all plantings in Australia! Murray can also be thanked for pioneering Pinot Noir. In 1979, his great friend and UK wine merchant, John Avery entered 1976 Tyrrell's Vat 6 Pinot Noir in the Wine Olympiad in Paris, making top wine in the world and the front page of the New York Times. Murray's tongue-in-cheek humour was popular; he sold a lot of great wine and slavishly spread the Tyrrell's name. It seems rather fitting therefore that the year of his death - 2000 - happened to be a particularly great vintage. Each Tyrrell generation has favoured and championed a different grape – Edward loved Shiraz, Murray pioneered Chardonnay and Murray's son Bruce who joined the company in 1974 is a great fan of Semillon.

02

The practise of maturing Vat 1 Semillon in old oak continued until 1990, when the process changed to stainless steel tanks. Bruce was convinced that Semillon had two facets - the first fresh and crisp, the second intense with age. He hid 1000 cases of the 1989 Vat 1 away from Murray's sight, releasing it years later when the toasty, honeyed qualities could shine through. Since then, Vat 1 has become one of the most awarded Show wines of all time with nearly 100 Trophies and countless gold medals to its name. Through judicious purchases, the family has 800 acres under vine today and alongside the Vat Series, Tyrrell's has developed an individual vineyard series of exceptional wines which includes Stevens (Shiraz and Semillon),

Belford (Chardonnay and Semillon), HVD (Semillon) and 4 Acres (Shiraz). Some of the vines in these wines date back to 1867 and are all pre-phylloxera making them very special creations. In 2008, Tyrrell's received 14 trophies at the Hunter Valley Wine Show, from the 19 presented. I remember it well, because I was the international judge that year.

The winery is a blend of ancient and modern; still holding the original press that Edward Tyrrell installed in 1863 for the Belford and Vat 47 Chardonnays. Chief winemaker Andrew Spinaze has worked with Bruce for over 30 years and red winemaker Mark Richardson has been on board for over 15. Bruce and his

wife Pauline work in the business with their children Chris, Jane and John, and this academy has spawned the likes of illustrious winemakers like Drew Noon, Andrew Thomas, Andrew Margan, Trevor Jones and Ben Glaetzer. This is a family business that commands incredible respect and influence.

03   *View looking south over the Short Flat and 4 Acre vineyards to the winery*

04   *Edward Tyrrell's original Ironbark slab hut*

05   *Cutting the cake in the 1860's Hand Press*

Clonakilla

• The Clonakilla estate may only date back 40 or so years but its impact has been staggering. The Clonakilla Vineyard (meaning meadow of the church) was established in 1971 by John Kirk on a 44-acre farm near the village of Murrumbateman, north of Canberra and his son Tim is now the resident winemaker there. Tim is a passionate fan of Rhône wines and it was his tour of the Rhône, back in 1991, that inspired him to blend Viognier with his well-established Shiraz vines. This started the trend for Australian Shiraz/Viognier blends and suddenly Clonakilla's wines were on everyone's lips.

Highly sought-after by restaurateurs and private collectors alike, these are some of the most sensual reds in the country. Tim has also made a different red cuvée simply called Syrah which is modelled on Hermitage, in order to complement his already fanatically followed paean to Côte-Rôtie. This estate is already a superstar, and I am certain that those wine lists and cellars in which Clonakilla wines doesn't sit alongside Guigal, Clape and Chave will put this oversight right.

New Zealand

Felton Road

"Felton Road owner Nigel Greening and winemaker Blair Walter redefine the meaning of meticulous work; analysing and scrutinising every last detail."

Central Otago
South Island
Established 1991

| 01

• Every estate in this book is a master of their craft, but Felton Road owner Nigel Greening and winemaker Blair Walter redefine the meaning of meticulous work; analysing and scrutinising every last detail. These two self-deprecating chaps are ultra-perfectionists with wizard skills, extensive global wine knowledge and stellar palates. In just over a decade they have made Felton Road the most famous producer in New Zealand and, along with fellow iconic alumnus Ata Rangi, they were awarded the inaugural Tipuranga Teitei o Aotearoa or 'Grand Cru of New Zealand' in 2010.

The property was established in 1991 by Stewart Elms (referenced by the Elm tree on the label) and the first wines were released in 1997. Elms determined that the north-facing slopes at the end of Felton Road, in the Bannockburn ward of Central Otago, were the warmest and most suited to growing and making world-class wines in the region. He could not have been more accurate.

Nigel Greening, an ex creative guru from England, bought the business in 2000 and he has expanded on this theme. The vineyards were converted to organic farming from 2001 onwards, and since 2010, they have full biodynamic accreditation. The tending of vines is done entirely by hand with cover crops planted between the rows to assist in controlling vine vigour, to improve soil health and to encourage biodiversity. This is a core belief

of Felton Road's and as the vines mature the wines are becoming some of the most captivating on the planet.

There are three distinct vineyard sites from which Felton Road draws fruit - The Elms, Cornish Point and Calvert. Cornish Point is an old gold mining settlement where the first large find was made in the Central Otago gold rush. It was named after the Cornish miners who worked there, and after being abandoned in the late 19th century, it was planted to apricots. Felton Road developed this site and planted it with vines in 2000. With 18 different clone and rootstock combinations, separated into 25 distinct blocks, this is a Pinot Noir fanatics' playground. Calvert vineyard is 1 km east of The Elms vineyard and winery. Planted in three phases between 1999 and 2003 with Pinot Noir, Chardonnay and Riesling; fruit is taken from this vineyard by Craggy Range (q.v.) and also Mike Weersing at Pyramid Valley. It is one of the first vineyards in New Zealand that works to a

Burgundian model; dividing up the land between different winemakers.

Felton Road has made its name as a Pinot Noir specialist, but I must mention the sublime white wines made here, too. There are three Rieslings, from driest to sweetest - Dry Riesling, Riesling and Block 1 Riesling. All are sensational and you can pick the appropriate one out of the wine rack to suit your mood or cooking. I have always favoured the middle cuvée, simply called Riesling; regularly giving it a half point more (out of 20) in my notes. If I had to choose just one this would be the wine, but I don't and nor should you. These are wines full of life and character and they all have a terrific, sleek chassis and magnificent length.

The Chardonnays, too, are phenomenal, starting with Bannockburn Chardonnay, which is a very attractive, minimally oaked wine (only 10% new oak). Block 2 Chardonnay, from The Elms vineyard, is a slightly richer wine, designed to age for

longer, but it again, is not at all bruised by excessive oaking. The respect for the raw materials, and desire to protect the integrity and source of the fruit is to be applauded at Felton Road. The wines themselves sing and they couldn't be from anywhere else, which is the primary aim of ultra-high

01 Just a sign for some, but the culmination of a pilgrimage for many visitors

02 Calvert vineyard, with the Kawarau River in the background

quality, boutique wine estates. Five Pinot Noirs complete the picture and there is not a finer, nor more fascinating range of wines outside of Burgundy. Bannockburn Pinot is the most forward-drinking wine and it is the largest production, too.

This is the wine that is responsible for Felton Road gaining the top five-star listing in my Great New Zealand Pinot Noir Classification. This wine is the embodiment of balance and harmony and from this stunning starting point the other four wines fan out; focusing on their exact vineyard sites and peculiarities. Cornish Point comes from its namesake vineyard, as does Calvert, while Block 3 and Block 5 are specific 'lieu-dits' in The Elms vineyard, on the Felton Road property. I will not describe the intricate differences in these wines in

this book, preferring to point you to my website and articles on specific vintages and tasting notes. However you must know that Blair and Nigel strain every sinew, and do everything possible not to lose any molecules of complexity and originality in these five wines. They are the direct vinous expression of the vineyards that they tend every day of their lives, and they all taste absolutely awesome. Nothing can be more rewarding than making wines like this. Perhaps that is why they are such content, generous, gregarious and engaging people.

| 04

| 05

03 Felton Road's winery and tasting room,
    nestled among the vines

04 Looking north through The Elms: Block 3
    is just beyond the water, Block 5 to its right,
    with Block 2 beyond

05 The hard Bannockburn winters play an
    important role in minimising disease and
    pests

Pegasus Bay

"Pegasus is the symbol of wisdom, poetry and inspiration – all of these traits and more are found in Pegasus Bay wines."

Waipara
South Island
Established 1986

| 01

• I only heard about the wines of Pegasus Bay when I was the international judge at the Air New Zealand Awards, in Auckland, in 2004. It was here that I met Lynnette Hudson, winemaker at Pegasus Bay, and in one evening's chat, I understood why the wines of Peg Bay taste like they do – her enthusiasm and passion for wine is unrivalled. Over the years she and her husband Mat Donaldson, also a winemaker at their family company, have become good friends. It is rare to meet people in the wine business who are brutally honest about their wines and who also have an unlimited thirst for tasting new wines and improving their own at every opportunity. I have subsequently visited the winery and conducted vast vertical tastings with Lynnette and Mat, and I am blown away by their all-encompassing knowledge of their soils, their stellar wines and finely-honed skills.

Pegasus Bay winery is situated in the Waipara Valley in the South Island. To the east, it is separated from the ocean (and Pegasus Bay itself) by a range of hills which protects them from the freezing Pacific winds. To the west you find the Southern Alps (or Main Divide – the other wine label in the company) and this is where the warm winds rise. This precise site gives Pegasus Bay Winery its warm days and cool nights – the time-honoured recipe for fine, ripe, elegant wine.

The Donaldson family members are all involved in their business and their skills are extremely complementary. Ivan Donaldson pioneered grape growing and wine making in the region in the 70s. He is an associate professor and consultant neurologist by training, but his love of wine inspired him to start the Pegasus Bay operation. Day-to-day, he oversees the meticulous viticulture on the estate; leading a large band of highly skilled workers. His wife Christine, runs the grounds which are immaculate. She is an opera nut and you will see this reflected in the names of their top wines. Wine tourism is extremely important here and the Donaldsons take great pride in their restaurant, and the synergy between their menus and their wines. Their eldest son, Mat, studied oenology and viticulture at Roseworthy College, in Australia and Lynnette did the same at Lincoln University in New Zealand. They have both worked abroad, in particular in Burgundy, and this valuable experience is evident in every sip of their wines.

Edward, another son, runs the marketing while his wife, Belinda, supervises the fabulous restaurant. Youngest son, Paul, works as General Manager for the company - so you can see that they have all of the bases covered.

I have long-tipped Waipara as one of the most important regions in New Zealand and it is this company, along with a couple of others that has inspired me to make this prediction. The minerality, the intricate layers of fruit and sheer class in the Pegasus Bay wines is staggering. What's more, they manage to make Riesling, Sauvignon Blanc, Semillon, Cabernet, Merlot, Chardonnay, Pinot Noir, and also sweet wines to extraordinarily high levels. This means they have cracked a lot of disparate disciplines in one very special location. My favourite wines at Pegasus Bay are the Chardonnays and Pinot Noirs – harking back to Mat and Lynnette's penchant for Burgundies, and also my own obsession with these varieties. I

also buy and collect their other wines however. The Sauvignon/Semillon blend is one of the most enchanting and ethereal styles in the world. It's fascinating to see that in a country obsessed with tutti-frutti Sauvignons, theirs is a dry, long, languid beast with no frills or embellishments. Their Dry Riesling is a triumph too, with rasping taut lime notes on the nose and mid-palate and a gentle, sherbet-kissed finish. The Merlot/Cabernet is grown in the warmer parts of the property and it is augmented with Cabernet Franc and Malbec to add complexity and aromatic notes.

01   *Pegasus Bay Pinot Noir*
02   *Pegasus Bay Vineyard*

This is one of New Zealand's finest Bordeaux blends and it ages like clockwork. The stars of the show are the Chardonnays and Pinot Noirs. All of the wines are released at estate level and also at special cuvée level. The Chardonnay and Pinot are model wines at Peg Bay showing restraint, elegance and complete understanding of what great wine should taste like. At special cuvée level, Virtuoso Chardonnay and Prima Donna Pinot Noir are sublime. It is the minerality underpinning the controlled, multi-faceted fruit which attracts me so strongly to these wines. They have density of flavour but also levity and gentleness; they are intricately built but silky smooth. Tasting back through the years at Pegasus Bay is as exciting as at any winery in the Côte d'Or. Aria is

the name for their late-picked Riesling, Maestro is the top Merlot/Cabernet, Finale is a botrytised Semillon and Encore is the same style but a Riesling. These are all beautiful and profound wines. Under the Pegasus Bay umbrella there is another set of wines called Main Divide. This used to be a second label style of set-up, but these days the wines have a distinct character of their own. I always head to the more widely available Pinot and Chardonnay to experience Lynnette and Mat's stardust winemaking at an affordable price. This family has pioneered winemaking in Waipara and I cannot commend them enough for this brave move. Pegasus is the symbol of wisdom, poetry and inspiration – all of these traits and more are found in Pegasus Bay wines.

03 *Entrance to Pegasus Bay*
04 *Pegasus Bay wine boxes*
05 *Noble Botrytis Riesling*

Cloudy Bay

"This wine put the word Sauvignon Blanc into our collective vocabulary and catapulted the Marlborough wine region onto the world stage."

Marlborough
South Island
Established 1985

| 01

• I will never forget the fuss around Cloudy Bay Sauvignon Blanc when I started my career in the wine business in 1987. The allocation given to the Barnes Wine Shop, where I worked, was 20 cases and we then divided them up into two or three bottle lots for our most loyal customers. The arrival of Cloudy Bay in store was a highlight in their vinous calendar and I was equally caught up in Cloudy Bay fervour. After all, this wine put the word Sauvignon Blanc into our collective vocabulary and catapulted the Marlborough wine region onto the world stage. None of the Loire white classics, like Sancerre or Pouilly-Fumé, mentioned the grape variety Sauvignon Blanc on the label. It therefore appeared that Cloudy Bay and a handful of other small producers 'owned' this intellectual property.

A few years later, in my first job as a wine buyer, I listed this same wine at Bibendum Restaurant and it sold like hotcakes. A friend of mine came up with the idea of 'Cloudy Bay Watch', which I relayed on my weekly wine show on BBC Radio. The switchboard was deluged with calls from keen oenophiles asked to quote the highest Cloudy Bay Sauvignon restaurant price in town. From memory, the Dorchester topped the list at just under £50 – unthinkable at the time for any Pouilly-Fumé or Sancerre! Cloudy Bay appeared on wine brokers' lists alongside Grand Cru Burgundies and blue chip clarets and was growing in popularity.

Twenty five years later there are hundreds of Marlborough producers all making Sauvignon Blanc and Cloudy Bay's pioneering status has largely been forgotten by today's legion of Sauvignon fans.

I would therefore like to redress the balance by giving this pioneering winery a well-earned place in this book. The brainchild of David Hohnen, owner of Cape Mentelle in Margaret River, Western Australia, this whacky scheme came about when he tasted a Marlborough 'Savvy' and was bowled over by its flavours. He felt compelled to make a wine from this relatively untested region. He employed Kevin Judd as the man on the ground in Marlborough and they used the best fruit they could find.

The romantic label and evocative name (which Captain Cook came up with in 1770 when he cruised around the South Island's shores) combined with knockout, piercing citrus and elderflower fruit and a mesmerising aroma, all hypnotised the fanatical CB followers. A complete portfolio of wines joined the Sauvignon in due course. A stunning Chardonnay was, and still is, one of the finest in the country. A daring oaked Sauvignon Blanc, called Te Koko (the Maori name for Cloudy Bay), started a world-wide craze.

Many winemakers had been using oak as a subtle flavour enhancer and mid-palate builder, but Te Koko took this to a new level, emulating the unhinged wines of Didier Dagueneau, in the Loire, to great effect. A dramatic Pinot Noir, to my mind deserving more praise than the Sauvignon, has made great gains in the last few years. Pelorus, the excellent sparkler that's always been the market leader in New Zealand, (along with a few aromatic and sweet wines, that are harder to find internationally) completes the picture. Cloudy Bay was bought by LVMH and it is run by the drinks division arm of Moët Hennessy. Hohnen and Judd still make wine in their respective countries under their own labels and they can be justly proud of what they started. These days the Cloudy Bay wines are distributed widely and this takeover has been very good for Cloudy Bay. Clearly volumes have increased for Cloudy Bay Sauvignon Blanc but there is still not enough to satisfy the global demand. It is the Chardonnay and Pinot Noir which really grab my interest these days, but in an ocean of Sauvignon Blanc, Cloudy Bay still evokes powerful memories, backed up by mouth-watering flavours.

01   *Cloudy Bay Sauvignon Blanc*
02   *View over Cloudy Bay vineyard*

Ata Rangi

"This lyrically-named estate inspired me to come up with The Great New Zealand Pinot Noir Classification."

Martinborough
North Island
Established 1980

01

01   *Ata Rangi's welcome sign*
02   *Ata Rangi's vineyard with Rimutaka Ranges in background*

career that month. Funnily enough I was probably one of the first people in the UK to taste Ata Rangi wines, but not because we stocked them on our shelves. Alison Paton, co-owner of Ata Rangi worked as a sales assistant at the same little shop as I did back then, and she gave me a half-bottle of Ata Rangi Gewurztraminer as a present when she left to continue her travels around the world. I loved the wine and never forgot the name. The first Ata Rangi Pinot Noir was made in 1985 and I remember buying the first vintage imported into the UK a few years later – I just had to taste it and I wasn't disappointed.

Twenty years on and this lyrically-named estate inspired me to come up with The Great New Zealand Pinot Noir Classification (which Tyson Stelzer and I publish every year). Ata Rangi and three other exemplary estates sit at the top of the ladder with five stars. Ata Rangi, meaning Dawn Sky, was planted with the legendary gumboot clone of Pinot Noir by Alison's brother Clive in the early 80s. The story goes that an illegal cutting of Pinot Noir was taken from Domaine de la Romanée Conti's vineyards (another estate in this century of greats) and smuggled into New Zealand. It was impounded at customs and a bright member of staff, Malcolm Abel, recognising its importance, sent it to be 'looked after' at the state-owned viticulture station. Abel planted his own vineyard with cuttings from this material and Clive worked a vintage with him in 1982.

• The wine world was much smaller and less complicated in April 1987. I say this because I remember only a few New Zealand brands on the shelves of the wonderful little independent wine merchant in south west London where I started my

Sadly, Abel died unexpectedly, but he had allowed Clive to use this plant material and I am certain that he would have been amazed at the results. Augmented by a wide selection of other Pinot clones, the wines made here are nothing short of sublime. Martinborough is a small wine region, accounting for only 1% of New Zealand's wine production, but it makes an enormous noise on the international stage.

Sixty-five kilometres north east of Wellington, it takes one and a half hours to drive there from the City over the Rimutaka Ranges. The climate is Burgundian and the rain shadow cast by the Rimutaka and Tararua Ranges make it a relatively dry haven for grape growing. The Martinborough Terrace is the prime turf here – only one kilometre wide and five long it is where the majority of the top estates are found. At its heart is Ata Rangi and the flagship Pinot Noir is considered by many critics and wine connoisseurs to be New Zealand's finest. I

was lucky enough to be sitting on the Ata Rangi table at a Pinot Noir conference in Wellington in 2010, with Phyll Pattie, Clive's other half, and winemaker extraordinaire Helen Masters when they were awarded inaugural Tipuranga Teitei o Aotearoa or 'Grand Cru of New Zealand' to rapturous applause.

In addition to the main Ata Rangi Pinot, another Pinot is made here called Crimson which I heartily recommend and which features on many of the restaurant lists that I curate. In addition to these wines a sensual, spicy Merlot/Cabernet/Syrah blend called Célèbre is made. I used to struggle with this wine, but recent vintages have given me immense pleasure. Lismore Pinot Gris is one of the country's finest PGs with line and length and pliable, billowing fruit, while Craighall Chardonnay is a challenging, starkly mineral wine with lime pith, strident oak and a bracing finish. A few other releases are not regularly exported, so I

don't see them that often, but this is also a good thing because they give you and me a reason to go and visit Ata Rangi in person. One noteworthy addendum to this wonderfully Pinot-drenched entry is the Paton family's commitment to conservation. It is interesting to note that many people featured in this book appreciate how lucky they are to be working the very special soils in their vineyards, and by dint of their successes they give something back to help the planet.

02

| 03

Clive Paton's obsessive desire to repopulate his region's tree-plundered terrain is to be admired. He has focused his efforts on protecting and re-establishing New Zealand's iconic red-flowering Rata - a mighty tree, once prolific in New Zealand. This tree was largely torched by early settlers and the remaining stands are now threatened by the rampant brush-tailed possum. These pests were introduced in 1837 to establish a fur trade, but they kill rata trees by their thousands and decimate indigenous bird populations, too. Project Crimson was set up to protect these trees from this vermin and this is why Ata Rangi uses the name on one of its wines to highlight this movement. With Clive's help The Bush Block, previously barren scrub land, has been replanted with thousands of native trees and shrubs. A further 130ha of land is protected by the Department of Conservation and this too has been planted with thousands more trees. A winegrower's relationship with his surroundings is fundamental to either's perceived success. This is beautifully demonstrated by the Paton family at Ata Rangi. Indeed in the Queen's Birthday Honours of 2012, Clive was appointed an Officer of the New Zealand Order of Merit.

04

05

Craggy Range

"These inspirational surroundings have made this winery and its superb cellar door, restaurant and cottages a favourite destination for serious wine lovers."

Hawke's Bay
North Island
Established 1997

| 01

• When entrepreneur Terry Peabody put down his roots, his family didn't expect them to be literal. Running companies all over the world, this Brisbane-based magnate, with the 'Midas touch', decided wine would be a great legacy for his children to inherit. A fortuitous meeting with Steve Smith MW (New Zealand's first specialist viticulturist Master of Wine) convinced him that New Zealand was the location for his dream and that a world class, multi-regional, single vineyard specialist wine company was the way forward. Having previously worked as a viticulturalist for a large New Zealand wine company, Steve had knowledge of hundreds of plots of land across the country. He and Terry hatched a plan to create one of the most exciting new brands in the world.

Based in Hawke's Bay, Giants Winery - the home of Craggy Range - is at the base of the spectacular scarp of Te Mata Peak. These inspirational surroundings have made this winery and its superb cellar door, restaurant and cottages a favourite destination for serious wine lovers. Drawing on fruit from Martinborough and Hawke's Bay in the North Island, and Central Otago and Marlborough in the South Island, this company takes a masterful approach to its craft.

Only single vineyard wines are allowed and styles include Sauvignon Blanc, Riesling, Chardonnay, Pinot Noir, Syrah and what they call Gimblett Gravels blends,

which can include Cabernet Sauvignon, Merlot, Malbec and Petit Verdot. Since Steve's Craggy Range journey started, he and his team have been on or near the top of all of his chosen vinous disciplines. I have tasted virtually every wine produced under this label and here is the fabulous roll-call. The Family Collection wines are sensational, starting with two contrasting Sauvignon Blanc – Avery Vineyard from Marlborough and Te Muna Road Vineyard from Martinborough, both of which are gripping. A delicate but beautiful Riesling, also from Te Muna Road Vineyard, is a joy. A rare, brooding Gimblett Gravels Chardonnay is partnered with a racy, mineral-soaked Kidnappers Vineyard Chardonnay, which is tempered by the sea breeze at Te Awanga. The two Pinot Noirs are completely different, with the Calvert Vineyard version, from arguably the most famous Pinot vineyard in the country, from Central Otago – sensual and all-encompassing. The Te Muna Road Vineyard Pinot, from Martinborough is upright and blessed with pristine cherry notes.

The Gimblett Gravels region, of which 100ha (out of a total of 850) is owned by Craggy Range is home to some mighty reds. Te Kahu is usually a Merlot-dominant blend featuring varying amounts of Cabernet Franc, and Sauvignon and Malbec depending on the vintage. This wine inevitably keeps you guessing! The Merlot is not 100% but prefers to employ both Cabernets and sometimes Malbec to layer complexity. Gimblett Gravels Vineyard Syrah uses a splash of Viognier to heighten its aromatics in true Northern Rhône style.

Above this series of exemplary wines you'll find the Prestige Collection wines. Les Beaux Cailloux Chardonnay, from the Gimblett Gravels, will stop being made after the 2011 vintage, so track down a bottle before it disappears – it is sublime. Aroha is the top Pinot Noir from the Te Muna Road Vineyard and it is one of the most vital and beautiful of the modern Pinots from New Zealand. With briary blueberry notes and a fair degree of whole bunch fermentation, this is a wine that sets

out to rival not just the local competition but everything around the world, too.

Sophia is another Gimblett Gravels red blend, this time a Merlot-dominant wine with increasing Cabernet content. A gradual drop in alcohol levels and new oak content make it more refined than in years gone by. Finally, Le Sol is the top Syrah in the country and staggeringly well made. Craggy Range will surely maintain its trajectory of excellence and with a portfolio of wines covering virtually every style, you are sure to fall under its charms if you haven't already done so.

01 *Craggy Range Gimblett Gravels Syrah*
02 *Early morning at the home of Craggy Range, Giants Winery*

California

Spottswoode

"The Novaks, who own this 40-acre family winegrowing estate, are some of the most discreet, modest, passionate, skilful and environmentally responsible people in the business."

Napa Valley
Established 1882

Cabernets are the antithesis of the hectic, showy, oft-gaudy wines made in the Valley. The Novaks, who own this 40-acre family winegrowing estate, are some of the most discreet, modest, passionate, skilful and environmentally responsible people in the business.

The original 31-acre estate was established back in 1882 by George Schonewald and he named it Esmeralda. He built the historic Victorian house (shown on the Spottswoode label) which was inspired by Hotel Del Monte, in Monterey, where he used to work. He designed a stunning garden and planted a 17-acre vineyard. He sold a slice of land adjacent to the property to Frank Kraft, who built a farmhouse as well as a magnificent stone wine cellar – remember this point for later on. After Schonewald's wife died he sold the property to Joseph Bliss and in 1908 Bliss sold to Dr. George Allen who renamed the estate Lyndenhurst – a name which appears on one of the wines today.

Two years later Mrs. Albert Spotts settled here and renamed the property Spottswoode in memory of her late husband. Grapes continued to be grown here throughout Prohibition, supplying the St. Helena Cooperative, from which Gallo purchased most of what was crushed. Mrs. Spotts gifted the property to her niece Florence Holmes, who lived there with her daughter and grand-children until, in 1972, the present owner Mary Novak and her

01   *A bottle of the Spottswoode Cabernet, on which the historic estate home is depicted*
02   *A view of the Estate Cabernet Sauvignon through the majestic Canary Island palms*

• There is something eminently distinguished about the Spottswoode set up. I have followed these wines for two decades and not once have I witnessed anything other than elegance and integrity in the wines. In some ways the Spottswoode

husband Dr. Jack Novak bought Spottswoode and raised their five children there.

Fired with a new-found enthusiasm for wine, the Novaks bought a further 15 acres and this is the estate we know today. They set about replanting the vineyard with Cabernet Sauvignon, Zinfandel and Sauvignon Blanc. Then, suddenly, Jack tragically passed away and Mary made the brave decision to soldier on alone and pursue their shared dream. She sold grapes to the Duckhorn and Shafer families among others and, in 1982, she released her first Spottswoode Cabernet Sauvignon, exactly 100 years after the estate's founding. Tony Soter was brought in as winemaker and they decided to graft over the Zinfandel to Cabernet Franc and Merlot.

In 1985 they undertook an organic viticultural regime, which at the time was considered to be radical; reflecting the property and its unique soil and setting

in the wines. In 1987 Beth Novak, the youngest daughter, took on the presidency of Spottswoode. An economics graduate with experience in the wine trade, too, she fast became a fervent spokesperson for sustainable viticulture and she and Mary took the estate to a new level of creativity and professionalism. Phylloxera, the vine root-eating louse, started its march (or rather munch) through the Valley, wreaking havoc, and so Spottswoode started its own vine replanting programme with earnest.

In 1989, they bought the Kraft property next door (serendipity working perfectly) and renovated the beautiful old pre-Prohibition barn, making it into a new barrel hall and office. I remember meeting the Novaks back in the early 90s when I was touring Napa. The 1991 'Tenth anniversary release' Estate Cabernet Sauvignon had a profound effect on me, and I made sure that Spottswoode Cabernet won a place on Bibendum Restaurant's

wine list (one of the restaurant wine lists that I look after in London) from that day onwards. A woman named Pam Starr made their wines from 1992-1996, with Tony Soter consulting. In 1997 Rosemary Cakebread took over from Pam Starr as winemaker, continuing in the same vein, replanting judiciously and working organically with Jennifer Williams joining as assistant winemaker in 2002. This period for me marked an increased layering in flavour and grace in the wines which took the Spottswoode Cabernet to a new level. I was pouring this wine at my wine schools and masterclass dinners, and wine lovers would stare in disbelief at the glass when I told them it was a Napa Cabernet. I suppose that this was because we were conditioned to think that the wines from this Cabernet

02

stronghold would be overwhelmingly oaky (as many are), but the relief and adoration for this wine shown by my audiences was incredible when they learned the truth and the name. I remember seeing Mary again in 2004 and marvelling at her boundless energy and stunning elegance – both characteristics always found in her wines.

In 2005, a Lyndenhurst Cabernet was released (the 2002 vintage) using younger vine fruit from the replanted material and those barrels which didn't quite 'fit' into the Estate wine. It was met with rave reviews only equalled with immense frustration as production was, and is, tiny! Jennifer took over the helm as winemaker followed by Aron Weinkauf who succeeded as

winemaker in 2011. With Lindy Novak, Beth's sister, overseeing marketing, the Novak ladies masterminded a successful recruitment drive of passionate wine lovers to the Spottswoode cause. 2012 is the 40th anniversary of the Novaks owning this great estate, the 30th anniversary of its first wine, the 25th anniversary of Beth joining Mary, the 20th anniversary of it being certified organic and Lindy joining the firm and also Mary's 80th birthday. You are unlikely to meet anyone as focused, passionate and holistically enlightening in the wine world as Mary Novak, so make sure that you endeavour to track down one of her family's rare wines and toast her and Jack's gift to the wine world.

03   *Barrels of the Spottswoode Cabernet aging in the pre-Prohibition barrel cellar*

04   *Beth Novak Milliken, Lindy and Mary Novak of Spottswoode*

05   *Spottswoode Estate home*

Shafer

"It is a rare talent for one winery to be so proficient at a wide range of disciplines, but Shafer manages to amaze."

Napa Valley
Established 1972

| 01

01 *Hillside Select, Shafer Vineyards' signature Cabernet Sauvignon, is sourced from the winery's estate vineyards in the Stags Leap District of Napa Valley*

02 *The winery welcomes visitors by appointment to taste its current vintages in a setting designed to integrate the sights, sounds, and scents of the surrounding vineyards.*

• I first visited the Napa Valley in the early 90s on an official Napa Valley Vintners-sponsored wine tour for young members of the UK wine trade. I remember loving this tour more than any other of that period. The enthusiasm, professionalism and 'joie de vivre' of the Napa superstar winemakers was a wonder to behold. Obviously Cabernet was (and is) King and yet the diversity of wines on show, the famous characters' humility and generosity and the stunning scenery itself was an unforgettable eye-opener. I met countless heroes, but there is one family which left an indelible mark both on my soul and palate - the Shafer father and son team at their Stag's Leap District stronghold.

John Shafer retired from publishing back in 1972 and he decided to romantically dive into the wine business, buying a 210-acre estate in Napa Valley's Stags Leap District. Most people who do this simply fail, while others fail to make a profit and they limp along. A very rare group of people succeed in this life change and this is because they are fully wedded to the project; working night and day to make it happen and picking the right 'dirt' in which to work. John is part of the latter and with typical commitment and passion, replanted the old vineyards at the property and terraced the precipitous hillsides, creating a stunning estate.

The first vintage came in 1978 and Shafer made only 1,000 cases of wine. The 1978 Cabernet was a legendary wine and it blew local competition away in a San Francisco Vintners Club event. It also trounced a handful of First Growth Bordeaux in an international blind tasting held in Germany in 1993, and instantly put the Shafer name on the global wine stage. John's son, Doug,

became the winemaker in 1983 and was joined by an assistant winemaker, Elias Fernandez whose story is a fascinating one. Elias graduated from U.C. Davis as an oenologist after having spent his youth working in various Napa vineyards with his father, who was a Mexican farm labourer. Elias initially showed a remarkable aptitude for music and gained a scholarship to attend the University of Nevada, Reno to study jazz. After a year he returned to his family roots however and changed courses to study winemaking at U.C. Davis. One can only imagine the seismic shift needed to make this transition. Thank goodness he did because with his help, the Shafers have made some of the most profound Californian wines that I have ever tasted.

The vineyards have been developed and expanded over the years and now Shafer boasts sites in the Oak Knoll, Stag's Leap and Carneros districts. The winery has grown too, and there are incredible and extensive caves carved into the hillside, giving them perfect barrel and bottle ageing conditions.

Elias was appointed head winemaker in 1994 when Doug took over the reins as president of the company. John became chairman of the board and it must have been an incredible moment for him. Just over 20 years into his new job he had already achieved some stunning successes. His team was complete and the consolidation and finessing period

then began. It is a rare talent for one winery to be so proficient at a wide range of disciplines, but Shafer manages to amaze not only with its serious red wines, but also with 'Red Shoulder Ranch' – its epic Chardonnay coming from a 70-acre property in Carneros. This is a ripe, rich, sultry wine with masses of charm overlaying a stunning mineral chassis. You would expect a Cabernet specialist to dabble with Merlot, but Shafer doesn't treat this difficult variety as a second-class citizen. Instead, it lavishes it with attention and ensures that the fruit is intense, but fresh and harvested without it becoming too jammy or porty. This may fly in the face of

highly rated Merlots from other producers, but it certainly makes sure that the wine is balanced, age-worthy and also downright delicious. A second bottle of Merlot is also within mere mortals' grasp such is the controlled alcohol on display in this wine – and this is a rare statement these days. 'One Point Five' is a Stags Leap District Cabernet Sauvignon named after John and Doug's combined generational input to their creation. Made from fruit predominantly sourced from the Hillside Estate surrounding the winery, as well as a 25-acre vineyard two miles away called Borderline, this is a more forward- drinking Cabernet than the flagship wine. 'Relentless' is a wine named after Elias's relentless pursuit of perfection and is a smoky, meaty, hedonistic Syrah/ Petite Sirah blend which comes from a remote ridge-top vineyard in the southern foothills of Napa Valley's Vaca Mountain range. The star of the show at Shafer is 'Hillside Select'. This Cabernet is picked from a very low-yielding amphitheatre-shaped vineyard dotted with rock and only bearing a foot or two of volcanic topsoil. The warm days and cold nights, thanks to its aspect, geographical peculiarities and proximity to San Francisco Bay, mean that the grapes here are sensationally complex, small and packed with intense mineral and fruit notes. Unsurprisingly this is one of the world's most revered and slavishly followed Cabernet Sauvignon wines. For a company that generates all of its power needs with solar energy and that always sticks to its first family principles, it is my great honour to include it and its jaw-droppingly impressive wines to this 100.

03 *Harvests are carried out at night to ensure that the fruit is crushed in cool, pristine condition.*

04 *The red wines mature in new French oak barrels in Shafer caves. Hillside Select is in barrel for three years, then another year in the bottle prior to release.*

05 *The vineyards are surrounded by the Cabernet Sauvignon vines which are the source of Hillside Select.*

Ridge

• Paul Draper joined Ridge in 1969 by which time this estate already had an 80-year pedigree of making wine at the Monte Bello winery. Ridge hit the headlines when its 1971 Monte Bello Cabernet performed extremely well against stern French opposition in a tasting known as the Judgement of Paris, in 1976. I tasted at the 35th anniversary re-enactment of this event and the same wine came top. The 2000 vintage also triumphed in a younger flight of wines. Draper is one of the world's most talented and inspirational wine pioneers. Drawing fruit from different and distinct sources, Ridge is also the preeminent producer of Zinfandel blends in the world. Geyserville, in the Alexander Valley, and Lytton Springs, in the Dry Creek Valley, made from field blends of Zin and other ancient vines, are a permanent fixture on all of the wine lists that I work on.

Au Bon Climat

• Jim Clendenen was supposed to have been a lawyer, but a gap year tour around Europe resulted in him stopping off in Burgundy for a month, and to some extent he is still there! The confluence of a highly intelligent and thirsty man and France's greatest Chardonnays and Pinot Noirs had a profound effect on him. On his return to California, he moved into the wine business and launched ABC in 1982. He sources incredible fruit from top-flight vineyards in the State and crafts stunning wines in a sun-kissed Burgundian model. Every wine in his portfolio hits the spot and I regularly pour his sensual Pinots to highlight just how complex and subtle Californian Pinot can be. His Isabelle Pinot Noir cuvée is one of the most alluring wines that you could ever hope to taste.

Argentina

Bodega Catena Zapata

"These are considered to be Argentina's most profound wines and I still feel that Catena has even more success ahead of it with wines as memorable and profound as any on the planet."

Mendoza
Established 1902

| 01

• With no other Argentinean or Chilean estates in this book, Bodega Catena Zapata is out on its own, largely because pioneering is what Nicolás Catena has done all of his life, putting world class Argentinean wine on the map. As well as being a pioneer, he is also a thinker and a doer. His family has helped him, too, as have well-chosen consultants but it is one man who has taken his bulk-wine producing estate to the edge of the stratosphere in just forty years and this is his story.

Nicolás' grandfather, Nicola, left Italy for Argentina in 1898. He planted his first vines in Mendoza in 1902, favouring the Malbec grape which seemed to ripen well, but internationally was more familiar as a blending component, and certainly not a star performer in the wines of Bordeaux. He had faith that this stalwart and unglamorous grape would do well in the sunny, dusty, virgin land. The estate flourished and his son Domingo developed it into one of the largest in the region, supplying bulk wine to a thirsty market.

By the 1960s Argentina's economy had taken a turn for the worse and Domingo had to make heart-breaking and difficult decisions regarding his business. There was even the question, one year, of whether or not it was even worth picking the grapes such was the dismal outlook. His son, Nicolás, a gifted mathematician, had just received a PhD in Economics, but put his academic career on ice; deciding to join the family firm after his grandfather and mother tragically died in a car crash. Nicolás decided to concentrate on growing their customer base in spite of a very difficult climate. This work, raising the profile of the estate, bottling their own blends and introducing the Catena brand to the market in the late '60s and '70s paid dividends. At this time Catena was fortunately, regularly, invited to the Argentinean Consulate to discuss export strategies and there he was poured Châteaux Lafite, Latour and Margaux – these flavours inspired him greatly. An academic at heart, Nicolás decided to take up an offer as Visiting Scholar in Economics at the University of California, Berkeley. It was at this time that Nicolás discovered new and exciting styles of wine while rambling around the Napa Valley with his wife Elena.

These tastings led to meetings with great winemakers, like Robert Mondavi, and he was convinced that his family operation in Mendoza could raise the bar from table wines to world class wines. Times were tough with the outbreak of the Falklands War, but he returned to Argentina and sold his table wine company, only keeping Bodegas Esmeralda to make his intended fine wines. Argentina had no record of making fine wine, and yet he was driven to plant Cabernet, Chardonnay and Malbec at much higher altitudes than ever before. Despite the poor soils his persistence paid off, as the quality of the fruit harvested was sublime. With strict irrigation utilising Andean water, he could minutely control the quality of this fruit and the harvest dates, drawing them out to engender more complexity in the bunches.

When Domingo died in 1989 Nicolás threw himself into proving that his father was right about his hunch that Malbec could rival the great wines of Bordeaux. In 1994 he made his first Catena Malbec. I remember these wines being launched in the UK. I was mesmerised with the purity and layers of fruit which they had, but unusually for Argentinean Malbec they didn't have the coarseness and astringency so often associated with this swarthy variety. Cabernet Sauvignon was performing well, too, and in 1994 he bottled a small batch from the oldest vines, calling it Catena Alta Cabernet. It was slippery, deep, lusty and multi-layered – clearly inspired by his time in California. With French Chardonnay clones giving him excellent results in his high altitude Tupungato vineyards he again amazed the critics, by producing silky smooth, classy wines not dissimilar to a fine Californian Chardonnay and in the 1995, Catena Alta Chardonnay was born. Catena Alta Malbec followed in 1996

01 *Nicolás Catena Zapata 2008*
02 *Bodega Catena Zapata Winery*

| 02

showcasing the finest fruit from the harvest. The following year Nicolás Catena and José Galante, his winemaker since 1975, were rewarded with a stunning Cabernet crop. Nicolás was inspired to create a top cuvée which he named 1997 Nicolás Catena Zapata (Zapata is his mother's maiden name); a blend of 95% Cabernet Sauvignon and 5% Malbec. He toured the world hosting a series of comparative tastings with this wine, pitching it against First Growth clarets and top Californian Cabernets to rave reviews and this cemented the Catena reputation forever in the eyes of the world's most discerning collectors.

Nicolás has continued to research and develop his wines aided by his son Ernesto and daughter Laura. A total of 145 different clones of Malbec were planted in the La Pirámide vineyard; the five best used to determine the best soil and altitude combinations for success. Over the years they have sought advice from Paul Hobbs, the superb Californian winemaker, and also Jacques Lurton, of Bordeaux fame. In 2004 a series of three spectacular new Malbecs were created using the incredible fruit from the Nicasia and Adrianna Vineyards (between 1.2 and 1.5km above sea level). These are considered to be Argentina's most profound wines and I still feel that Catena has even more success ahead of it with wines as memorable and profound as any on the planet.

03 *Domingo Catena with his parents, sisters and brothers*

04 *Barrel Cellar Room*

05 *Nicolás Catena Zapata Cellar Room*

Directory

ALAIN GRAILLOT
Les Chênes Verts
26600 Pont-de-l'Isère
Drôme Rhône-Alpes
France
Tel + 33 (0) 4 75 84 67 52

ALLEGRINI
Via Giare 9/11
37022 Fumane di Valpolicella
Italy
Tel +39 045 68 32 011
Info@allegrini.it
allegrini.it

ARGIANO
S. Angelo in Colle
53024 Montalcino
Italy
Tel +39 05 77 84 40 37
argiano@argiano.net
argiano.net

ATA RANGI
14 Puruatanga Road P. O. Box 43
Martinborough 5741
New Zealand
Tel +64 (0)6 30 69 570
wines@atarangi.co.nz
atarangi.co.nz

AU BON CLIMAT
P.O. Box 113
Los Olivos,
CA 93441
USA
Tel +1 805 937 9801
info@aubonclimat.com
aubonclimat.com

AUGUSTE CLAPE
146, Avenue Colonel Rousset
07130 Cornas
France
Tel +33 (0) 4 75 40 59 51

BEAUCASTEL
Chemin de Beaucastel
84350 Courthezon
France
Tel +33 (0) 4 90 70 41 00
familleperrin@beaucastel.com
beaucastel.com

BILLECART-SALMON
40, Rue Carnot
B.P 8
51160 Mareuil-sur-Aÿ
France
Tel + 33 (0) 3 26 52 60 22
champagne-billecart.fr

BLANDY'S SGPS, LDA.
Avenida Zarco, 32
PO Box 408
9001-956 Funchal
Madeira, Portugal
Tel +351 291 200 600
info@blandy.com
blandy.com

BODEGAS HIDALGO LA GITANA
Banda de la Playa, 42
11540 Sanlúcar de Barrameda
Cádiz
Spain
Tel +34 956 385 304
bodegashidalgo@lagitana.es
lagitana.es

BOEKENHOUTSKLOOF
Boekenhoutskloof Winery
P.O. Box 433
Excelsior Road
Franschhoek 7690
South Africa
Tel +27 (0) 21 876 3320
info@boekenhoutskloof.co.za
boekenhoutskloof.co.za

CHAMPAGNE BOLLINGER
20, Blvd du Marechal de Lattre de
Tassigny
51160 Aÿ, Champagne
France
Tel +33 (0) 3 26 53 33 66
p.petry@champagne-bollinger.fr
bollinger.fr

CASTELLO DEL TERRICCIO
Localita Terriccio
56040 Castellina Marittima
Pisa
Italy
Tel +39 05 06 99 709
terriccio.it

CASTELLO DI FONTERUTOLI
Via Ottone III di Sassonia n°5
Loc. Fonterutoli
I-53011 Castellina in Chianti
Italy
Tel +39 05 77 73 571
mazzei.it/eng_154

CATENA ZAPATA
J. Cobos s/n, Agrelo
Luján de Cuyo
Mendoza
Argentina
Tel +54 (261) 413 1100
catenawines.com

M. CHAPOUTIER
18 Avenue Dr. Paul Durand
B.P. 38
26600 Tain-l'Hermitage
France
Tel +33 (0) 4 75 08 92 61
chapoutier.com

CHÂTEAU AUSONE
33330 Saint-Emilion
France
Tel +33 (0) 5 57 24 24 57
chateau-ausone.fr

CHÂTEAU CHEVAL BLANC
33330 Saint-Emilion
France
Tel +33 (0) 5 57 55 55 55
chateau-cheval-blanc.com

CHÂTEAU CLIMENS
33720 Barsac
France
Tel +33 (0) 5 56 27 15 33
contact@chateau-climens.fr
chateau-climens.fr

CHÂTEAU D'YQUEM
33210 Sauternes
France
Tel +33 (0) 5 57 98 07 07
yquem.fr

CHÂTEAU HAUT-BRION
135 Avenue Jean Jaures
33608 Pessac
France
Tel +33 (0) 5 56 00 29 30
haut-brion.com

CHÂTEAU LAFITE ROTHSCHILD
33250 Pauillac
France
Tel +33 (0) 5 53 89 78 00
visites@lafite.com
lafite.com

CHÂTEAU LATOUR
Saint-Lambert
33250 Pauillac
France
Tel +33 (0) 5 56 73 19 80
chateau-latour.com

CHÂTEAU LÉOVILLE-LAS CASES
33250 Saint-Julien-Beychevelle
France
Tel +33 (0) 5 56 73 25 26

CHÂTEAU MARGAUX
33460 Margaux
France
Tel +33 (0) 5 57 88 83 83
chateau-margaux.com

- CHÂTEAU PÉTRUS
33500 POMEROL
FRANCE

- CHÂTEAU PONTET-CANET
33250 PAUILLAC
FRANCE
TEL + 33 (0) 5 56 59 04 04
INFO@PONTET-CANET.COM
PONTET-CANET.COM

- CHÂTEAU RIEUSSEC
33210 FARGUES DE LANGON
FRANCE
TEL +33 (0) 5 53 89 78 00
RIEUSSEC@LAFITE.COM
LAFITE.COM

- CHÂTEAU THIVIN
69460 ODENAS
FRANCE
TEL +33 (0) 4 74 03 47 53
CHATEAU-THIVIN.COM

- CLONAKILLA
3 CRISPS LANE
MURRUMBATEMAN NSW 2582
AUSTRALIA
TEL +61 (02) 6227 5877
WINE@CLONAKILLA.COM.AU
CLONAKILLA.COM.AU

- CLOUDY BAY
JACKSONS ROAD (P.O. BOX 376)
BLENHEIM
NEW ZEALAND 7240
TEL +64 (0) 35 20 91 40
INFO@CLOUDYBAY.CO.NZ
CLOUDYBAY.CO.NZ

- CRAGGY RANGE
253 WAIMARAMA ROAD
P.O. BOX 8749
HAVELOCK NORTH
NEW ZEALAND
TEL +64 (0) 68 73 71 26
INFO@CRAGGYRANGE.COM
CRAGGYRANGE.COM

- CULLEN WINES
4323 CAVES ROAD
WILYABRUP WA 6280
AUSTRALIA
TEL +61 (08) 9755 5277
PA@CULLENWINES.COM.AU
CULLENWINES.COM.AU

- DOMAINE ARMAND ROUSSEAU
1, RUE DE L'AUMÔNERIE
21220 GEVREY-CHAMBERTIN
FRANCE
TEL +33 (0) 3 80 34 30 55
CONTACT@DOMAINE-ROUSSEAU.COM
DOMAINE-ROUSSEAU.COM

- DOMAINE BERNARD BAUDRY
9, COTEAU DE SONNAY
37500 CRAVANT LES COTEAUX
FRANCE
TEL + 33 (0) 2 47 93 15 79
CHINON.COM/VIGNOBLE/BERNARD-BAUDRY

- DOMAINE BONNEAU DU
MARTRAY
21420 PERNAND-VERGELESSES
FRANCE
TEL +33 (0) 3 80 21 50 64
BONNEAUDUMARTRAY.COM

- DOMAINE JEAN-FRANÇOIS
COCHE-DURY
9, RUE CHARLES-GIRAUD
21190 MEURSAULT
FRANCE
TEL +33 (0) 3 80 21 24 12

- DOMAINE COMTE GEORGES DE
VOGÜÉ
7, RUE STE BARBE
21220 CHAMBOLLE-MUSIGNY
FRANCE
TEL +33 (0) 3 80 62 86 25

- DOMAINE DES COMTES LAFON
5, RUE PIERRE JOIGNEAUX
21190 MEURSAULT
FRANCE
TEL +33 (0) 3 80 21 22 17
COMTES.LAFON@GMAIL.COM
COMTES-LAFON.FR

- DOMAINE LEFLAIVE
PLACE DES MARRONNIERS
21190 PULIGNY-MONTRACHET
FRANCE
TEL +33 (0) 3 80 21 30 13
LEFLAIVE.FR

- DOMAINE MÉO-CAMUZET
11, RUE DES GRANDS CRUS
21700 VOSNE-ROMANEE
FRANCE
TEL +33 (0) 3 80 61 55 55
MEO-CAMUZET.COM

- DOMAINE PONSOT
21, RUE DE LA MONTAGNE
21220 MOREY-SAINT-DENIS
FRANCE
TEL +33 (0) 3 80 34 32 46
INFO@DOMAINE-PONSOT.COM
DOMAINE-PONSOT.COM

- DOMAINE RAMONET
4, PLACE NOYERS
21190 CHASSAGNE-MONTRACHET
FRANCE
TEL +33 (0) 3 80 21 30 88

- DOMAINE RAVENEAU
9, RUE DE CHICHEE
89800 CHABLIS
YONNE, BOURGOGNE
FRANCE

- DOMAINE DE LA ROMANÉE
CONTI
1 RUE DERRIÈRE LE FOUR
21700 VOSNE-ROMANÉE
FRANCE
TEL + 33 (0) 3 80 62 48 80

- DOMAINE G. ROUMIER
RUE DE VERGY
21220 CHAMBOLLE-MUSIGNY
FRANCE
TEL +33 (0) 3 80 62 86 37
ROUMIER.COM

- DOMAINE DU VIEUX TÉLÉGRAPHE
3, ROUTE DE CHÂTEAUNEUF-DU-PAPE
84370 BEDARRIDES
FRANCE
TEL +33 (0) 4 90 33 00 31
VIGNOBLES@BRUNIER.FR
VIEUXTELEGRAPHE.COM

- DOMAINE RENÉ + VINCENT
DAUVISSAT
8, RUE EMILE ZOLA
89800 CHABLIS
FRANCE

- DR. LOOSEN
ST. JOHANNISHOF
D-54470 BERNKASTEL-KUES
GERMANY
TEL +49 (0) 65 31 34 26
INFO@DRLOOSEN.COM
DRLOOSEN.COM

- ELIO ALTARE
FRAZIONE ANNUNZIATA, 51
12064 LA MORRA (CN)
ITALY
TEL +39 0173 50835
ELIOALTARE@ELIOALTARE.COM
ELIOALTARE.COM

ETIENNE SAUZET
11, RUE DE POISEUL
21190 PULIGNY-MONTRACHET
FRANCE
TEL +33 (0) 3 80 21 32 10
ETIENNESAUZET.COM

FELTON ROAD
BANNOCKBURN, R.D.
CENTRAL OTAGO 9384
NEW ZEALAND
TEL +64 (0) 34 45 08 85
WINES@FELTONROAD.COM
FELTONROAD.COM

FILLIATREAU
49400 SAUMUR
FRANCE
TEL +33 (0) 2 41 52 90 84
DOMAINE@FILLIATREAU.FR
FILLIATREAU.FR

FRANÇOIS COTAT
CHAVIGNOL
18300 SANCERRE
FRANCE
TEL +33 (0) 2 48 54 21 27

FRANZ HIRTZBERGER
KREMSERSTRASSE 8,
3620 SPITZ
AUSTRIA
TEL +43 (0) 27 13 22 09
WEINGUT@HIRTZBERGER.COM
HIRTZBERGER.AT

GAJA
VIA TORINO 36
12050 BARBARESCO
ITALY
TEL +39 0173 635255
GAJA.COM

GEORGES VERNAY
1, ROUTE NATIONALE
69420 CONDRIEU
FRANCE
TEL +33 (0) 4 74 56 81 81
PA@GEORGES-VERNAY.FR
GEORGES-VERNAY.FR

W & J GRAHAM'S & CA.
RUA REI RAMIRO, 514
4400 VILA NOVA DE GAIA
PORTUGAL
TEL +351 22 377 64 84/85
GRAHAMS@GRAHAMSPORTLODGE.COM
GRAHAMS-PORT.COM

GROSSET
P O BOX 64
AUBURN SA 5451
CLARE VALLEY
SOUTH AUSTRALIA
TEL +61 8 8849 2175
INFO@GROSSET.COM.AU
GROSSET.COM.AU

E. GUIGAL
CHÂTEAU D'AMPUIS
69420 AMPUIS
FRANCE
TEL+33 (0) 4 74 56 10 22
GUIGAL.COM

HUET
11, RUE DE LA CROIX BUISÉE
BP 34
37210 VOUVRAY
FRANCE
TEL +33 (0) 2 47 52 78 87
CONTACT@HUET-ECHANSONNE.COM
HUET-ECHANSONNE.COM

ISOLE E OLENA
ISOLE 1, 50021 BARBERINO VAL D'ELSA
ITALY
TEL +39 055 807 2767

JEAN-LOUIS CHAVE
37, AVENUE ST-JOSEPH
07300 MAUVES
FRANCE
TEL +33 (0) 4 75 08 24 63

JIM BARRY
CRAIG HILL ROAD
CLARE SA 5453
AUSTRALIA
TEL +61 (0) 8 88422261
JBWINES@JIMBARRY.COM
JIMBARRY.COM

JOH. JOS. PRÜM
UFERALLEE 19
D-54470 BERNKASTEL-WEHLEN
GERMANY
TEL +49 (0) 65 31 30 91
INFO@JJPRUEM.COM
JJPRUEM.COM

KARTHÄUSERHOF
54292 TRIER – EITELSBACH
GERMANY
TEL +49 (0) 651 5121
MAIL@KARTHAEUSERHOF.COM
KARTHAEUSERHOF.COM

LEEUWIN ESTATE
STEVENS RD, MARGARET RIVER
6285 WESTERN AUSTRALIA
TEL +61 (0) 8 9759 0000
WINERY@LEEUWINESTATE.COM.AU
LEEUWINESTATE.COM.AU

CHAMPAGNE LOUIS ROEDERER
21, BOULEVARD LUNDY
51053 REIMS
FRANCE
TEL +33 (0) 3 26 40 42 11
COMO@CHAMPAGNE-ROEDERER.COM
FACEBOOK.COM/LOUISROEDEREROFFICIAL
TWITTER @_LOUISROEDERER_
CHAMPAGNE-ROEDERER.COM

MARCEL DEISS
15, ROUTE DU VIN
68750 BERGHEIM
FRANCE
TEL +33 (0) 3 89 73 63 37
MARCELDEISS@MARCELDEISS.FR
MARCELDEISS.COM

MIGUEL TORRES
M. TORRES, 6
08720 VILAFRANCA DEL PENEDÈS
BARCELONA
SPAIN
WEBMASTER@TORRES.ES
TORRES.ES

MORIC
A-7051 GROSSHÖFLEIN
KIRCHENGASSE 3
TEL +43 (0) 664 400 32 31
MORIC.AT

OREMUS
BAJCSY - SZ. ÚT.
45 TOLCSVA H-3934
HUNGARY
TEL +36 (0) 47 38 45 05
TOKAJOREMUS@TOKAJOREMUS.HU
TOKAJOREMUS.COM

ORNELLAIA
LOCALITÀ ORNELLAIA, 191
FRAZ. BOLGHERI 57022
CASTAGNETO CARDUCCI (LI)
ITALY
TEL +39 0565 718 11
ORNELLAIA.COM

PEGASUS BAY
STOCKGROVE RD, WAIPARA
RD 2 AMBERLEY 7482
NORTH CANTERBURY
NEW ZEALAND
TEL +64 (0) 33 14 68 61
INFO@PEGASUSBAY.COM
PEGASUSBAY.COM

PENFOLDS
77 SOUTHBANK BOULEVARD
SOUTHBANK
VIC 3006
AUSTRALIA
TEL +61 (0) 3 96 33 20 00
PENFOLDS.COM

- **PETER LEHMANN**
  Para Road or PO Box 315
  Tanunda
  South Australia 5352
  Tel +61 (0) 8 85 65 95 00
  cellar.door@peterlehmannwines.com
  peterlehmannwines.com.au

- **PIEROPAN**
  Via Camuzzoni 3
  37038 Soave
  Verona
  Italy
  Tel +39 04 56 19 01 71
  info@pieropan.it
  pieropan.it/it

- **LE PIN**
  Thienpont Gerard et Jacques
  Lotissements Grands Champs
  33500 Pomerol
  France
  Tel +33 (0) 5 57 51 33 99

- **PLANETA**
  Contrada Dispensa
  92013 Menfi (AG)
  Sicily
  Italy
  Tel +39 09 25 80 0 09
  planeta.it

- **PODERI ALDO CONTERNO**
  12065 - Monforte d'Alba Loc. Bussia, 48
  Piemonte
  Italy
  Tel +39 0173 78150
  poderialdoconterno.com

- **POLIZIANO**
  Via Fontago
  1-53040 Montepulciano Stazione
  Italy
  Tel +39 05 78 73 81 71
  info@carlettipoliziano.com
  carlettipoliziano.com

- **CHAMPAGNE POL ROGER**
  1, Rue Henri Le Large
  B.P 199
  51206 Epernay Cedex
  France
  Tel +33 (0) 3 26 59 58 00
  polroger@polroger.fr
  polroger.com

- **QUINTA DO NOVAL VINHOS**
  Av. Diogo Leite, 256
  4400 - 111 Vila Nova de Gaia
  Portugal
  Tel +351 22 3770270
  noval@quintadonoval.pt
  quintadonoval.com

- **RIDGE**
  17100 Monte Bello Road
  Cupertino,
  CA 95014
  USA
  Tel +1 408 867 3233
  Wine@ridgewine.com
  ridgewine.com

- **LA RIOJA ALTA**
  Avda. de Vizcaya, 8
  26200 Haro
  La Rioja
  Spain
  Tel +34 941 310 346
  riojalta@riojalta.com
  riojalta.com

- **RUSTENBERG**
  Rustenberg Rd.
  Stellenbosch 7600
  South Africa
  Tel +27 (21) 809 1200
  wine@rustenberg.co.za
  rustenberg.co.za

- **SADIE FAMILY WINES**
  P.O. Box 1019
  Aprilskloof Road
  7299 Paardeberg
  Malmesbury
  South Africa
  Tel +27 (0) 2 24 82 31 38
  thesadiefamily.com

- **SASSICAIA**
  Tenuta San Guido
  Loc. Le Capanne 27
  I-57022
  Bolgheri, Livorno
  Italy
  Tel+39 0565 762003
  info@sassicaia.com
  sassicaia.com

- **SHAFER**
  6154 Silverado Trail
  Napa
  CA 94558
  USA
  Tel +1 707 944 2877
  info@shafervineyards.com
  shafervineyards.com

- **LA SPINETTA**
  Via Annunziata 17
  14054 Castagnole Lanze
  Italy
  Tel +39 0141 877396
  info@la-spinetta.com
  la-spinetta.com

- **SPOTTSWOODE**
  1902 Madrona Avenue
  St. Helena
  CA 94574
  USA
  Tel +1 707 963 0134
  estate@spottswoode.com
  spottswoode.com

- **LA TAILLE AUX LOUPS**
  8, rue des Aîtres
  37270 Husseau
  Montlouis-sur-Loire
  France
  Tel +33 (0) 2 47 45 11 11
  jackyblot.fr/taille_loups.php

- **TAYLOR'S**
  Rua do Choupelo, 250
  4400-088 Vila Nova de Gaia
  Portugal
  Tel +351 223 742 800
  taylor.pt

- **TEMPIER**
  1082, Chemin des Fanges
  83330 Le Plan du Castellet
  France
  Tel +33 (0) 4 94 98 70 21
  domaine.tempier@gmail.com
  domainetempier.com

- **TYRRELL'S**
  1838 Broke Road
  Pokolbin NSW 2320
  Australia
  Tel +61 (0) 2 49 93 70 00
  cellardoor@tyrrells.com.au
  tyrrells.com.au

- **VALDESPINO**
  Pozo del Olivar, 16
  Jerez de la Frontera
  Spain
  Tel +34 956 331 450
  grupoestevez.es/valdespino.com

- **VEGA-SICILIA**
  E-47359
  Valbuena de Duero
  Spain
  Tel +34 983 680 147
  vegasicilia@vega-sicilia.com
  vega-sicilia.com

- **VIEUX CHÂTEAU CERTAN**
  33500 Pomerol
  France
  Tel +33 (0) 5 57 51 17 33
  vieux-chateau-certan.com

- **WARRE'S**
  Travesa do Barão de Forrester,
  Apartado 26
  4401 Vila Nova de Gaia
  Portugal
  Tel +351 22 377 6300
  warre.com

- **WEINBACH**
  25, Route du Vin
  68240 Kaysersberg
  France
  Tel +33 (0) 3 89 47 13 21
  contact@domaineweinbach.com
  domaineweinbach.com

Acknowledgements
by Quintessentially Publishing

• **Matthew Jukes** has provided us with hours of fascinating and insightful reading with his heartfelt and descriptive language and personal experiences. Taste is similar to smell; any written description of an intangible element should logically pale when compared to the reality of the actual sensory experience. Matthew overcomes any obstacles created by words and passionately conveys the nuances and qualities of all the wines within these pages. Close your eyes and you can detect and savour every note as if you were breathing it in, and swirling it around your palate. Thank you to Matthew for sharing his unique and professional opinion of some of the finest wines on the planet; for setting the scene and also for recounting the human stories that have coloured and shaped these wines' existences.

We are also very thankful to a host of talented people at Quintessentially: **Christopher Rayner** for supporting the project and encouraging its development with utter faith; the team at **Quintessentially Wine** for offering their invaluable advice, guidance and friendship behind the scenes. **Lois Crompton** spent months fostering relationships with wine estates scattered across all corners of the globe, in order to include them in this book - a measure of endless persistence and patience. We are very grateful to her for this. Thank you to **Nathalie Grainger Bradbury** for editing the content throughout so as to maintain the flow on every single page, and so much more. **Will Sutton**, **Thomas Parker**, **Haydn Squibb** and **Katherine Klaben** brought invaluable help to the project as well as support and loyalty.

We are eternally thankful for the immense talent of **Giorgio Criscione** who breathed life into the design and feel of this book. His hours of painstaking labour and utter dedication are matched by his flawless professionalism and unwavering belief. We admire your talent and patience so much Giorgio!

Giorgio's colleagues at Quintessentially Design also brought us their help and dedication: thank you very much to **Chris Charalambous** who offered his time and photographic services along with **François Boutemy**, who kindly lent us his Studio Simulacra's services. **Julian Luskin** and **George Page** for their invaluable help. **Alessandra Agostini**, our wonderful Italian printer and her **EBS** team were the final piece of the jigsaw in producing this beautiful book.

Aaron Simpson, **Ben Elliot**, **Paul Drummond** and **Rebecca Tucker** backed the teams all the way.

"In wine one beholds the heart of another"
Anonymous

Quintessentially Publishing Ltd.
29 Portland Place, London, W1B 1QB
Tel +44 (0)20 3073 6845
info@quintessentiallypublishing.com
www.quintessentiallypublishing.com

ISBN: 978-0-9569952-2-3

For wine advice, membership enquiries or to purchase any
of the wines from these estates, please contact:

Quintessentially Wine Ltd.
29 Portland Place, London, W1B 1QB
Tel: +44 (0)845 224 9261
info@quintessentiallywine.com
www.quintesssentiallywine.com